CLIFFSCOMPLETE

Shakespeare's

King Henry IV, Part 1

About the Author
Michael McMahon (B.A.) (hons) (Dunelm) taught literature for many years in private and public schools and colleges in England. He now writes full-time, mostly on educational matters, and his work is frequently published in the English national press.

Publisher's Acknowledgments
Editorial
  Project Editor: Elizabeth Netedu Kuball
  Acquisitions Editor: Gregory W. Tubach
  Editorial Director: Kristin A. Cocks
  Special Help: Michelle Hacker
  Illustrator: DD Dowden
Production
  Indexer: Becky Hornyak
  Proofreader: Toni Settle
  IDG Books Indianapolis Production Department

CliffsComplete King Henry IV, Part 1
Published by
IDG Books Worldwide, Inc.
An International Data Group Company
919 E. Hillsdale Blvd.
Suite 400
Foster City, CA 94404
www.idgbooks.com (IDG Books Worldwide Web site)
www.cliffsnotes.com (CliffsNotes Web site)

Library of Congress Catalog Card No.: 00-01096

ISBN: 0-7645-8570-3

Printed in the United States of America

10 9 8 7 6 5 4 3 2 1

1O/SV/QU/QQ/IN

Distributed in the United States by IDG Books Worldwide, Inc.

Distributed by CDG Books Canada Inc. for Canada; by Transworld Publishers Limited in the United Kingdom; by IDG Norge Books for Norway; by IDG Sweden Books for Sweden; by IDG Books Australia Publishing Corporation Pty. Ltd. for Australia and New Zealand; by TransQuest Publishers Pte Ltd. for Singapore, Malaysia, Thailand, Indonesia, and Hong Kong; by Gotop Information Inc. for Taiwan; by ICG Muse, Inc. for Japan; by Intersoft for South Africa; by Eyrolles for France; by International Thomson Publishing for Germany, Austria and Switzerland; by Distribuidora Cuspide for Argentina; by LR International for Brazil; by Galileo Libros for Chile; by Ediciones ZETA S.C.R. Ltda. for Peru; by WS Computer Publishing Corporation, Inc., for the Philippines; by Contemporanea de Ediciones for Venezuela; by Express Computer Distributors for the Caribbean and West Indies; by Micronesia Media Distributor, Inc. for Micronesia; by Chips Computadoras S.A. de C.V. for Mexico; by Editorial Norma de Panama S.A. for Panama; by American Bookshops for Finland.

For general information on IDG Books Worldwide's books in the U.S., please call our Consumer Customer Service department at 800-762-2974. For reseller information, including discounts and premium sales, please call our Reseller Customer Service department at 800-434-3422.

For information on where to purchase IDG Books Worldwide's books outside the U.S., please contact our International Sales department at 317-596-5530 or fax 317-572-4002.

For consumer information on foreign language translations, please contact our Customer Service department at 1-800-434-3422, fax 317-572-4002, or e-mail rights@idgbooks.com.

For information on licensing foreign or domestic rights, please phone +1-650-653-7098.

For sales inquiries and special prices for bulk quantities, please contact our Order Services department at 800-434-3422 or write to the address above.

For information on using IDG Books Worldwide's books in the classroom or for ordering examination copies, please contact our Educational Sales department at 800-434-2086 or fax 317-572-4005.

For press review copies, author interviews, or other publicity information, please contact our Public Relations department at 650-653-7000 or fax 650-653-7500.

For authorization to photocopy items for corporate, personal, or educational use, please contact Copyright Clearance Center, 222 Rosewood Drive, Danvers, MA 01923, or fax 978-750-4470.

CLIFFSCOMPLETE

Shakespeare's

King Henry IV, Part 1

Edited by Sidney Lamb

Associate Professor of English

Sir George Williams University, Montreal

Complete Text + Commentaries + Glossary

Commentary by Michael McMahon

IDG BOOKS WORLDWIDE

IDG Books Worldwide, Inc.

An International Data Group Company

Foster City, CA • Chicago, IL • Indianapolis, IN • New York, NY

CLIFFSCOMPLETE

Shakespeare's

King Henry IV, Part 1

CONTENTS AT A GLANCE

CLIFFSCOMPLETE

Shakespeare's

King Henry IV, Part 1

TABLE OF CONTENTS

Shakespeare's

KING HENRY IV, PART 1

INTRODUCTION TO WILLIAM SHAKESPEARE

William Shakespeare, or the "Bard" as people fondly call him, permeates almost all aspects of our society. He can be found in our classrooms, on our televisions, in our theatres, and in our cinemas. Speaking to us through his plays, Shakespeare comments on his life and culture, as well as our own. Actors still regularly perform his plays on the modern stage and screen. The 1990s, for example, saw the release of cinematic versions of *Romeo and Juliet, Hamlet, Othello, A Midsummer Night's Dream,* and many more of his works.

In addition to the popularity of Shakespeare's plays as he wrote them, other writers have modernized his works to attract new audiences. For example, *West Side Story* places *Romeo and Juliet* in New York City, and *A Thousand Acres* sets *King Lear* in Iowa corn country. Beyond adaptations and productions, his life and works have captured our cultural imagination. The twentieth century witnessed the production of a play about two minor characters from Shakespeare's *Hamlet* in *Rosencrantz and Guildenstern Are Dead* and a fictional movie about Shakespeare's early life and poetic inspiration in *Shakespeare in Love.*

Despite his monumental presence in our culture, Shakespeare remains enigmatic. He does not tell us which plays he wrote alone, on which plays he collaborated with other playwrights, or which versions of his plays to read and perform. Furthermore, with only a handful of documents available about his life, he does not tell us much about Shakespeare the person, forcing critics and scholars to look to historical references to uncover the true-life great dramatist.

Anti-Stratfordians — modern scholars who question the authorship of Shakespeare's plays — have used this lack of information to argue that William Shakespeare either never existed or, if he did exist, did not write any of the plays we attribute to him. They believe that another historical figure, such as Francis Bacon or Queen Elizabeth I, used the name as a cover. Whether or not a man named

An engraved portrait of Shakespeare by an unknown artist, ca. 1607. Culver Pictures, Inc./SuperStock

William Shakespeare ever actually existed is ultimately secondary to the recognition that the group of plays bound together by that name does exist and continues to educate, enlighten, and entertain us.

Family life

Though scholars are unsure of the exact date of Shakespeare's birth, records indicate that his parents — Mary and John Shakespeare — baptized him on April 26, 1564, in the small provincial town of Stratford-upon-Avon — so named because it sat on the banks of the Avon river. Because common practice was to baptize infants a few days after they were born, scholars generally recognize April 23, 1564 as Shakespeare's birthday. Coincidentally, April 23 is the day of St. George, the patron saint of England, as well as the day upon which Shakespeare would die 52 years later. William was the third of Mary and John's eight children and the first of four sons. The house in which scholars believe Shakespeare to have been born stands on Henley Street and, despite many modifications over the years, you can still visit it today.

Shakespeare's father

Prior to Shakespeare's birth, John Shakespeare lived in Snitterfield, where he married Mary Arden, the daughter of his landlord. After moving to Stratford in 1552, he worked as a glover, a moneylender, and a dealer in agricultural products such as wool and grain. He also pursued public office and achieved a variety of posts including bailiff, Stratford's highest elected position — equivalent to a small town's mayor. At the height of his career, sometime near 1576, he petitioned the Herald's Office for a coat of arms and thus the right to be a gentleman. But the rise from the middle class to the gentry did not come right away, and the costly petition expired without being granted.

About this time, John Shakespeare mysteriously fell into financial difficulty. He became involved in serious litigation, was assessed heavy fines, and even lost his seat on the town council. Some scholars

Shakespeare's birthplace.
SuperStock

suggest that this decline could have resulted from religious discrimination because the Shakespeare family may have supported Catholicism, the practice of which was illegal in England. However, other scholars point out that not all religious dissenters (both Catholics and radical Puritans) lost their posts due to their religion. Whatever the cause of his decline, John did regain some prosperity toward the end of his life. In 1596, the Herald's Office granted the Shakespeare family a coat of arms at the petition of William, by now a successful playwright in London. And John, prior to his death in 1601, regained his seat on Stratford's town council.

Childhood and education

Our understanding of William Shakespeare's childhood in Stratford is primarily speculative because children do not often appear in the legal records from which many scholars attempt to reconstruct Shakespeare's life. Based on his father's local prominence, scholars speculate that Shakespeare most likely attended King's New School, a school that usually employed Oxford graduates and was generally well respected. Shakespeare would have started *petty school* — the rough equivalent to modern preschool — at the age of 4 or 5. He would have learned to read on a *hornbook*, which was a sheet of parchment or paper on which the alphabet and the Lord's Prayer were written. This sheet was framed in wood and covered with a transparent piece of horn for durability. After two years in petty school, he would have transferred to grammar school, where his school day would have probably lasted from 6 or 7 o'clock in the morning (depending on the time of year) until 5 o'clock in the evening, with only a handful of holidays.

While in grammar school, Shakespeare would primarily have studied Latin, reciting and reading the works of classical Roman authors such as Plautus, Ovid, Seneca, and Horace. Traces of these authors' works can be seen in his dramatic texts. Toward his last years in grammar school, Shakespeare would have acquired some basic skills in Greek as well. Thus the remark made by Ben Jonson, Shakespeare's well-educated friend and contemporary playwright, that Shakespeare knew "small Latin and less Greek" is accurate. Jonson is not saying that when Shakespeare left grammar school he was only semiliterate; he merely indicates that Shakespeare did not attend University, where he would have gained more Latin and Greek instruction.

Wife and children

When Shakespeare became an adult, the historical records documenting his existence began to increase. In November 1582, at the age of 18, he married 26-year-old Anne Hathaway from the nearby village of Shottery. The disparity in their ages, coupled with the fact that they baptized their first daughter, Susanna, only six months later in May 1583, has caused a great deal of modern speculation about the nature of their relationship. However, sixteenth-century conceptions of marriage differed slightly from our modern notions. Though all marriages needed to be performed before a member of the clergy, many of Shakespeare's contemporaries believed that a couple could establish a relationship through a premarital contract by exchanging vows in front of witnesses. This contract removed the social stigma of pregnancy before marriage. (Shakespeare's plays

contain instances of marriage prompted by pregnancy, and *Measure for Measure* includes this kind of premarital contract.) Two years later, in February 1585, Shakespeare baptized his twins Hamnet and Judith. Hamnet died at the age of 11 when Shakespeare was primarily living away from his family in London.

For seven years after the twins' baptism, the records remain silent on Shakespeare. At some point, he traveled to London and became involved with the theatre, but he could have been anywhere between 21 and 28 years old when he did. Though some have suggested that he may have served as an assistant to a schoolmaster at a provincial school, it seems likely that he went to London to become an actor, gradually becoming a playwright and gaining attention.

The plays: On stage and in print

The next mention of Shakespeare comes in 1592 by a University wit named Robert Greene when Shakespeare apparently was already a rising actor and playwright for the London stage. Greene, no longer a successful playwright, tried to warn other University wits about Shakespeare. He wrote:

> For there is an upstart crow, beautified with our feathers, that with his "Tiger's heart wrapped in a player's hide" supposes he is as well able to bombast out a blank verse as the best of you, and, being an absolute Johannes Factotum, is in his own conceit the only Shake-scene in a country.

This statement comes at a point in time when men without a University education, like Shakespeare, were starting to compete as dramatists with the University wits. As many critics have pointed out, Greene's statement recalls a line from *3 Henry VI*, which reads, "O tiger's heart wrapped in a woman's hide!" (I.4.137). Greene's remark does not indicate that Shakespeare was generally disliked. On the

A ground plan of London after the fire of 1666, drawn by Marcus Willemsz Doornik. Guildhall Library, London/AKG, Berlin/SuperStock

dramatic works, scholars believe that by this point he had written *The Two Gentlemen of Verona, The Taming of the Shrew,* the *Henry VI* trilogy, and *Titus Andronicus.* During his early years in the theatre, he primarily wrote history plays, with his romantic comedies emerging in the 1590s. Even at this early stage in his career, Shakespeare was a success. In 1597, he was able to purchase New Place, one of the two largest houses in Stratford, and secure a coat of arms for his family.

contrary, another University wit, Thomas Nashe, wrote of the great theatrical success of *Henry VI,* and Henry Chettle, Greene's publisher, later printed a flattering apology to Shakespeare. What Greene's statement does show us is that Shakespeare's reputation for poetry had reached enough of a prominence to provoke the envy of a failing competitor.

In the following year, 1593, the government closed London's theatres due to an outbreak of the bubonic plague. Publication history suggests that during this closure, Shakespeare may have written his two narrative poems, *Venus and Adonis,* published in 1593, and *The Rape of Lucrece,* published in 1594. These are the only two works that Shakespeare seems to have helped into print; each carries a dedication by Shakespeare to Henry Wriothesley, Earl of Southampton.

Stage success

When the theatres reopened in 1594, Shakespeare joined the Lord Chamberlain's Men, an acting company. Though uncertain about the history of his early

In 1597, the lease expired on the Lord Chamberlain's playhouse, called The Theatre. Because the owner of The Theatre refused to renew the lease, the acting company was forced to perform at various playhouses until the 1599 opening of the now famous Globe Theatre, which was literally built with lumber from The Theatre. (The Globe, later destroyed by fire, has recently been reconstructed in London and can be visited today.)

Recent scholars suggest that Shakespeare's great tragedy, *Julius Caesar,* may have been the first of Shakespeare's plays performed in the original playhouse. When this open-air theatre on the Thames River opened, financial papers list Shakespeare's name as one of the principal investors. Already an actor and a playwright, Shakespeare was now becoming a "Company Man." This new status allowed him to share in the profits of the theatre rather than merely getting paid for his plays, some of which publishers were beginning to release in quarto format.

Publications

A *quarto* was a small, inexpensive book typically used for leisure books such as plays; the term itself indicates that the printer folded the paper four times. The modern day equivalent of a quarto would be a paperback. In contrast, the first collected works of Shakespeare were in folio format, which means that the printer folded each sheet only once. Scholars call the collected edition of Shakespeare's works the *First Folio*. A folio was a larger and more prestigious book than a quarto, and printers generally reserved the format for works such as the Bible.

No evidence exists that Shakespeare participated in the publication of any of his plays. Members of Shakespeare's acting company printed the First Folio seven years after Shakespeare's death. Generally, playwrights wrote their works to be performed on stage, and publishing them was a novel innovation at the time. Shakespeare probably would not have thought of them as books in the way we do. In fact, as a principal investor in the acting company (which purchased the play as well as the exclusive right to perform it), he may not have even thought of them as his own. He would probably have thought of his plays as belonging to the company.

For this reason, scholars have generally characterized most quartos printed before the Folio as "bad" by arguing that printers pirated the plays and published them illegally. How would a printer have received a pirated copy of a play? The theories range from someone stealing a copy to an actor (or actors) selling the play by relating it from memory to a printer. Many times, major differences exist between a quarto version of the play and a folio version, causing uncertainty about which is Shakespeare's true creation. *Hamlet*, for example, is almost twice as long in the Folio as in quarto versions. Recently, scholars have come to realize the value of the different versions. The *Norton Shakespeare*, for example, includes all three versions of *King Lear* — the quarto, the folio, and the *conflated* version (the combination of the quarto and folio).

Prolific productions

The first decade of the 1600s witnessed the publication of additional quartos as well as the production of most of Shakespeare's great tragedies, with *Julius Caesar* appearing in 1599 and *Hamlet* in 1600–1601. After the death of Queen Elizabeth in 1603, the Lord Chamberlain's Men became the King's Men under James I, Elizabeth's successor. Around the time of this transition in the English monarchy, the famous tragedy *Othello* (1603–1604) was most likely written and performed, followed closely by *King Lear* (1605–1606), *Antony and Cleopatra* (1606), and *Macbeth* (1606) in the next two years.

Shakespeare's name also appears as a major investor in the 1609 acquisition of an indoor theatre known as the Blackfriars. This last period of Shakespeare's career, which includes plays that considered the acting conditions both at the Blackfriars and the open-air Globe Theatre, consists primarily of romances or tragicomedies such as *The Winter's Tale* and *The Tempest*. On June 29, 1613, during a performance of *All is True*, or *Henry VIII*, the thatching on top of The Globe caught fire, and the playhouse burned to the ground. After this incident, the King's Men moved solely into the indoor Blackfriars Theatre.

Final days

During the last years of his career, Shakespeare collaborated on a couple of plays with contemporary dramatist John Fletcher, even possibly coming out of retirement — which scholars believe began sometime in 1613 — to work on *The Two Noble Kinsmen* (1613–1614). Three years later, Shakespeare died on April 23, 1616. Though the exact cause of death remains unknown, a vicar from Stratford in the mid-seventeenth century wrote in his diary that Shakespeare, perhaps celebrating the marriage of his daughter, Judith, contracted a fever during a night of revelry with fellow literary figures Ben Jonson and Michael Drayton. Regardless, Shakespeare may have felt his death was imminent in March of that year, because he altered his will. Interestingly, his will mentions no book or theatrical manuscripts, perhaps indicating the lack of value that he put on printed versions of his dramatic works and their status as company property.

Seven years after Shakespeare's death, John Heminge and Henry Condell, fellow members of the King's Men, published his collected works. In their preface, they claim that they are publishing the true versions of Shakespeare's plays partially as a response to the previous quarto printings of 18 of his plays, most of these with multiple printings. This Folio contains 36 plays to which scholars generally add *Pericles* and *The Two Noble Kinsmen*. This volume of Shakespeare's plays began the process of constructing Shakespeare not only as England's national poet but also as a monumental figure whose plays would continue to captivate imaginations at the end of the millennium with no signs of stopping. Ben Jonson's prophetic line about Shakespeare in the First Folio — "He was not of an age, but for all time!" — certainly holds true.

Chronology of Shakespeare's plays

1590–1591	The Two Gentlemen of Verona
	The Taming of the Shrew
1591	2 Henry VI
	3 Henry VI
1592	1 Henry VI
	Titus Andronicus
1592–1593	Richard III
	Venus and Adonis
1593–1594	The Rape of Lucrece
1594	The Comedy of Errors
1594–1595	Love's Labour's Lost
1595	Richard II
	Romeo and Juliet
	A Midsummer Night's Dream
1595–1596	Love's Labour's Won
	(This manuscript was lost.)
1596	King John

1596–1597	The Merchant of Venice
	1 Henry IV
1597–1598	The Merry Wives of Windsor
	2 Henry IV
1598	Much Ado About Nothing
1598–1599	Henry V
1599	Julius Caesar
1599–1600	As You Like It
1600–1601	Hamlet
1601	Twelfth Night, or What You Will
1602	Troilus and Cressida
1593–1603	Sonnets
1603	Measure for Measure
1603–1604	A Lover's Complaint
	Othello
1604–1605	All's Well That Ends Well
1605	Timon of Athens
1605–1606	King Lear
1606	Macbeth
	Antony and Cleopatra
1607	Pericles
1608	Coriolanus
1609	The Winter's Tale
1610	Cymbeline
1611	The Tempest
1612–1613	Cardenio (with John Fletcher; this manuscript was lost.)
1613	All is True, or Henry VIII
1613–1614	The Two Noble Kinsmen (with John Fletcher)

This chronology is derived from Stanley Wells' and Gary Taylor's *William Shakespeare: A Textual Companion*, which is listed in the "Works consulted" section below.

A note on Shakespeare's language

Readers encountering Shakespeare for the first time usually find Early Modern English difficult to understand. Yet, rather than serving as a barrier to Shakespeare, the richness of this language should form part of our appreciation of the Bard.

One of the first things readers usually notice about the language is the use of pronouns. Like the King James Version of the Bible, Shakespeare's pronouns are slightly different from our own and can cause confusion. Words like "thou" (you), "thee" and "ye" (objective cases of you), and "thy" and "thine" (your/yours) appear throughout Shakespeare's plays. You may need a little time to get used to these changes. You can find the definitions for other words that commonly cause confusion in the "Notes" column on the right side of each page in this edition.

Iambic pentameter

Though Shakespeare sometimes wrote in prose, he wrote most of his plays in poetry, specifically blank verse. Blank verse consists of lines in unrhymed *iambic pentameter. Iambic* refers to the stress patterns of the line. An *iamb* is an element of sound that consists of two beats — the first unstressed (da) and the second stressed (DA). A good example of an iambic line is Hamlet's famous line "To be or not to be," in which you do not stress "To," "or," and "to," but you do stress "be," "not," and "be." *Pentameter* refers to the *meter* or number of stressed syllables in a line. *Penta*meter has five stressed syllables. Thus, Juliet's line "But soft, what light through yonder window breaks?" (II.2.2) is a good example of an iambic pentameter line.

Wordplay

Shakespeare's language is also verbally rich as he, along with many dramatists of his period, had a fondness for wordplay. This wordplay often takes the forms of double meanings, called *puns*, where a word can mean more than one thing in a given context. Shakespeare often employs these puns as a way of illustrating the distance between what is on the surface — *apparent* meanings — and what meanings lie underneath. Though recognizing these puns may be difficult at first, the glosses in the far right column point many of them out to you.

If you are encountering Shakespeare's plays for the first time, the following reading tips may help ease you into the plays. Shakespeare's lines were meant to be spoken; therefore, reading them aloud or speaking them should help with comprehension. Also, though most of the lines are poetic, do not forget to read complete sentences — move from period to period as well as from line to line. Although Shakespeare's language can be difficult at first, the rewards of immersing yourself in the richness and fluidity of the lines are immeasurable.

Works consulted

For more information on Shakespeare's life and works, see the following:

Bevington, David, ed. *The Complete Works of Shakespeare*. New York: Longman, 1997.

Evans, G.Blakemore, ed. *The Riverside Shakespeare*. Boston: Houghton Mifflin Co., 1997.

Greenblatt, Stephan, ed. *The Norton Shakespeare*. New York: W.W. Norton and Co., 1997.

Kastan, David Scott, ed. *A Companion to Shakespeare*. Oxford: Blackwell, 1999.

McDonald, Russ. *The Bedford Companion to Shakespeare: An Introduction with Documents*. Boston: Bedford-St. Martin's Press, 1996.

Wells, Stanley and Gary Taylor. *William Shakespeare: A Textual Companion*. New York: W.W. Norton and Co., 1997.

INTRODUCTION TO EARLY MODERN ENGLAND

William Shakespeare (1564–1616) lived during a period in England's history that people have generally referred to as the English Renaissance. The term *renaissance*, meaning rebirth, was applied to this period of English history as a way of celebrating what was perceived as the rapid development of art, literature, science, and politics: in many ways, the rebirth of classical Rome.

Recently, scholars have challenged the name "English Renaissance" on two grounds. First, some scholars argue that the term should not be used because women did not share in the advancements of English culture during this time period; their legal status was still below that of men. Second, other scholars have challenged the basic notion that this period saw a sudden explosion of culture. A rebirth of civilization suggests that the previous period of time was not civilized. This second group of scholars sees a much more gradual transition between the Middle Ages and Shakespeare's time.

Some people use the terms *Elizabethan* and *Jacobean* when referring to periods of the sixteenth and seventeenth centuries. These terms correspond to the reigns of Elizabeth I (1558–1603) and James I (1603–1625). The problem with these terms is that they do not cover large spans of time; for example, Shakespeare's life and career spans both monarchies.

Scholars are now beginning to replace Renaissance with the term Early Modern when referring to this time period, but people still use both terms interchangeably. The term *Early Modern* recognizes that this period established many of the foundations of our modern culture. Though critics still disagree about the exact dates of the period, in general, the dates range from 1450 to 1750. Thus, Shakespeare's life clearly falls within the Early Modern period.

Shakespeare's plays live on in our culture, but we must remember that Shakespeare's culture differed greatly from our own. Though his understanding of human nature and relationships seems to apply to our modern lives, we must try to understand the world he lived in so we can better understand his plays. This introduction helps you do just that. It examines the intellectual, religious, political, and social contexts of Shakespeare's work before turning to the importance of the theatre and the printing press.

Intellectual context

In general, people in Early Modern England looked at the universe, the human body, and science very differently from the way we do. But while we do not share their same beliefs, we must not think of people during Shakespeare's time as lacking in intelligence or education. Discoveries made during the Early Modern period concerning the universe and the human body provide the basis of modern science.

Cosmology

One subject we view very differently from Early Modern thinkers is cosmology. Shakespeare's contemporaries believed in the astronomy of Ptolemy, an intellectual from Alexandria in the second century A.D. Ptolemy thought that the earth stood at the center of the universe, surrounded by nine concentric rings. The celestial bodies circled the earth in the following order: the moon, Mercury, Venus, the sun, Mars, Jupiter, Saturn, and the stars. The entire system was controlled by the *primum mobile*, or Prime Mover, which initiated and maintained the movement of the celestial bodies. No one had yet discovered the last three planets in our solar system, Uranus, Neptune and Pluto.

In 1543, Nicolaus Copernicus published his theory of a sun-based solar system, in which the sun stood at the center and the planets revolved around it. Though this theory appeared prior to Shakespeare's birth, people didn't really start to change their minds until 1610, when Galileo used his telescope to confirm Copernicus' theory. David Bevington asserts in the general introduction to his edition of Shakespeare's works that during most of Shakespeare's writing career, the cosmology of the universe was in question, and this sense of uncertainty influences some of his plays.

Universal hierarchy

Closely related to Ptolemy's hierarchical view of the universe is a hierarchical conception of the Earth (sometimes referred to as the Chain of Being). During the Early Modern period, many people believed that all of creation was organized hierarchically. God existed at the top, followed by the angels, men, women, animals, plants, and rocks. (Because all women were thought to exist below all men on the chain, we can easily imagine the confusion that Elizabeth I caused when she became queen of England. She was literally "out of order," an expression that still exists in our society.) Though the concept of this hierarchy is a useful one when beginning to study Shakespeare, keep in mind that distinctions in this hierarchical view were not always clear and that we should not reduce all Early Modern thinking to a simple chain.

Elements and humors

The belief in a hierarchical scheme of existence created a comforting sense of order and balance that carried over into science as well. Shakespeare's contemporaries generally accepted that four different elements composed everything in the universe: earth, air, water, and fire. People associated these four elements with four qualities of being. These qualities — hot, cold, moist, and dry — appeared in different combinations in the elements. For example, air was hot and moist; water was cold and moist; earth was cold and dry; and fire was hot and dry.

In addition, people believed that the human body contained all four elements in the form of *humors* — blood, phlegm, yellow bile, and black bile — each of which corresponded to an element. Blood corresponded to air (hot and moist), phlegm to water (cold and moist), yellow bile to fire (hot and dry), and black bile to earth (cold and dry). When someone was sick, physicians generally believed that the patient's humors were not in the proper balance. For example, if someone were diagnosed with an abundance of blood, the physician would bleed the patient (using leeches or cutting the skin) in order to restore the balance.

Shakespeare's contemporaries also believed that the humors determined personality and temperament. If a person's dominant humor was blood, he was considered light-hearted. If dominated by yellow bile (or choler), that person was irritable. The dominance of phlegm led a person to be dull and kind. And if black bile prevailed, he was melancholy or sad. Thus, people of Early Modern England often used the humors to explain behavior and emotional outbursts. Throughout Shakespeare's plays, he uses the concept of the humors to define and explain various characters.

In *Henry IV, Part 1*, for example, the short temper and hot-headedness of Hotspur are classic symptoms of someone dominated by choler. After one of his angry outbursts (Act I, Scene 3) his father, Northumberland, explicitly accuses him of being "drunk with choler," and in Act III, Scene 1, Hotspur's wife tells him that he is "altogether governed by humors" — that is, moody.

Religious context

Shakespeare lived in an England full of religious uncertainty and dispute. From the Protestant Reformation to the translation of the Bible into English, the Early Modern era is punctuated with events that have greatly influenced modern religious beliefs.

The Reformation

Until the Protestant Reformation, the only Christian church was the Catholic, or "universal," church. Beginning in Europe in the early sixteenth century, religious thinkers such as Martin Luther and John Calvin, who claimed that the Roman Catholic Church had become corrupt and was no longer following the word of God, began what has become known as the Protestant Reformation. The Protestants ("protestors") believed in salvation by faith rather than works. They also believed in the primacy of the Bible and advocated giving all people access to reading the Bible.

Many English people initially resisted Protestant ideas. However, the Reformation in England began in 1527 during the reign of Henry VIII, prior to Shakespeare's birth. In that year, Henry VIII decided to divorce his wife, Catherine of Aragon, for her failure to produce a male heir. (Only one of their children, Mary, survived past infancy.) Rome denied Henry's petitions for a divorce, forcing him to divorce Catherine without the Church's approval, which he did in 1533.

The Act of Supremacy

The following year, the Pope excommunicated Henry VIII while Parliament confirmed his divorce and the legitimacy of his new marriage through the

A portrait of King Henry VIII, artist unknown, ca. 1542. National Portrait Gallery, London/SuperStock

Act of Succession. Later in 1534, Parliament passed the *Act of Supremacy*, naming Henry the "Supreme Head of the Church in England." Henry continued to persecute both radical Protestant reformers and Catholics who remained loyal to Rome.

Henry VIII's death in 1547 brought Edward VI, his 10-year-old son by Jane Seymour (the king's third wife), to the throne. This succession gave Protestant reformers the chance to solidify their break with the Catholic Church. During Edward's reign, Archbishop Thomas Cranmer established the foundation for the Anglican Church through his 42 articles of religion. He also wrote the first *Book of Common Prayer*, adopted in 1549, which was the official text for worship services in England.

Bloody Mary

Catholics continued to be persecuted until 1553, when the sickly Edward VI died and was succeeded by Mary, his half-sister and the Catholic daughter of Catherine of Aragon. The reign of Mary witnessed the reversal of religion in England through the restoration of Catholic authority and obedience to Rome. Protestants were executed in large numbers, which earned the monarch the nickname *Bloody Mary*. Many Protestants fled to Europe to escape persecution.

Elizabeth, the daughter of Henry VIII and Anne Boleyn, outwardly complied with the mandated Catholicism during her half-sister Mary's reign, but she restored Protestantism when she took the throne in 1558 after Mary's death. Thus, in the space of single decade, England's throne passed from Protestant to Catholic to Protestant, with each change carrying serious and deadly consequences.

Though Elizabeth reigned in relative peace from 1558 to her death in 1603, religion was still a serious concern for her subjects. During Shakespeare's life, a great deal of religious dissent existed in England. Many Catholics, who remained loyal to Rome and their church, were persecuted for their beliefs. At the other end of the spectrum, the Puritans were persecuted for their belief that the Reformation was not complete. (The English pejoratively applied the term *Puritan* to religious groups that wanted to continue purifying the English church by such measures as removing the *episcopacy,* or the structure of bishops.)

A portrait of Elizabeth I by George Gower, ca. 1588. National Portrait Gallery, London/SuperStock

The Great Bible

One thing agreed upon by both the Anglicans and Puritans was the importance of a Bible written in English. Translated by William Tyndale in 1525, the first authorized Bible in English, published in 1539, was known as the Great Bible. This Bible was later revised during Elizabeth's reign into what was known as the Bishop's Bible. As Stephen Greenblatt points out in his introduction to the *Norton Shakespeare,* Shakespeare would probably have been familiar with both the Bishop's Bible, heard aloud in Mass, and the Geneva Bible, which was written by English exiles in Geneva. The last authorized Bible produced during Shakespeare's lifetime came within the last decade of his life when James I's commissioned edition, known as the King James Bible, appeared in 1611.

Political context

Politics and religion were closely related in Shakespeare's England. Both of the monarchs under whom Shakespeare lived had to deal with religious and political dissenters.

Elizabeth I

Despite being a Protestant, Elizabeth I tried to take a middle road on the religious question. She allowed Catholics to practice their religion in private as long as they outwardly appeared Anglican and remained loyal to the throne.

Elizabeth's monarchy was one of absolute supremacy. Believing in the divine right of kings, she styled herself as being appointed by God to rule England. To oppose the Queen's will was the equivalent of opposing God's will. Known as *passive obedience,* this doctrine did not allow any opposition even to a tyrannical monarch because God had appointed the king or queen for reasons unknown to His subjects on earth. However, as Bevington notes, Elizabeth's power was not as absolute as her rhetoric suggested. Parliament, already well established in England, reserved some power, such as the authority to levy taxes, for itself.

Elizabeth I lived in a society that restricted women from possessing any political or personal autonomy and power. As queen, Elizabeth violated and called into question many of the prejudices and practices against women. In a way, her society forced her to "overcome" her sex in order to rule effectively. However, her position did nothing to increase the status of women in England.

One of the rhetorical strategies that Elizabeth adopted in order to rule effectively was to separate her position as monarch of England from her natural body — to separate her *body politic* from her *body natural*. In addition, throughout her reign, Elizabeth brilliantly negotiated between domestic and foreign factions — some of whom were anxious about a female monarch and wanted her to marry — appeasing both sides without ever committing to one.

She remained unmarried throughout her 45-year reign, partially by styling herself as the Virgin Queen whose purity represented England herself. Her refusal to marry and her habit of hinting and promising marriage with suitors both foreign and domestic helped Elizabeth maintain internal and external peace. Not marrying allowed her to retain her independence, but it left the succession of the English throne in question. In 1603, on her deathbed, she named James VI, King of Scotland and son of her cousin Mary, as her successor.

James I

When he assumed the English crown, James VI of Scotland became James I of England. (Some historians refer to him as James VI and I.) Like Elizabeth, James was a strong believer in the divine right of kings and their absolute authority.

Upon his arrival in London to claim the English throne, James made his plans to unite Scotland and England clear. However, a long-standing history of enmity existed between the two countries. Partially as a result of this history and the influx of Scottish courtiers into English society, anti-Scottish prejudice abounded in England. When James asked Parliament for the title of "King of Great Britain," he was denied.

As scholars such as Bevington have pointed out, James was less successful than Elizabeth was in negotiating between the different religious and political factions in England. Although he was a Protestant, he began to have problems with the Puritan sect of the House of Commons, which ultimately led to a rift between the court (which also started to have Catholic sympathies) and the Parliament. This rift between the monarchy and Parliament eventually escalated into the Civil War that would erupt during the reign of James's son, Charles I.

In spite of its difficulties with Parliament, James's court was a site of wealth, luxury, and extravagance. James I commissioned elaborate feasts, masques, and pageants, and in doing so he more than doubled the royal debt. Stephen Greenblatt suggests that Shakespeare's *The Tempest* may reflect this extravagance through Prospero's magnificent banquet and accompanying masque. Reigning from 1603 to 1625, James I remained the King of England throughout the last years of Shakespeare's life.

Social context

Shakespeare's England divided itself roughly into two social classes: the aristocrats (or nobility) and everyone else. The primary distinctions between these two classes were ancestry, wealth, and power. Simply put, the aristocrats were the only ones who possessed all three.

Aristocrats were born with their wealth, but the growth of trade and the development of skilled professions began to provide wealth for those not born with it. Although the notion of a middle class did not begin to develop until after Shakespeare's death, the possibility of some social mobility did exist in Early Modern England. Shakespeare himself used the wealth gained from the theatre to move into the lower ranks of the aristocracy by securing a coat of arms for his family.

Shakespeare was not unique in this movement, but not all people received the opportunity to increase their social status. Members of the aristocracy feared this social movement and, as a result, promoted harsh laws of apprenticeship and fashion, restricting certain styles of dress and material. These laws dictated that only the aristocracy could wear certain articles of clothing, colors, and materials. Though enforcement was a difficult task, the Early Modern aristocracy considered dressing above one's station a moral and ethical violation.

The status of women

The legal status of women did not allow them much public or private autonomy. English society functioned on a system of patriarchy and hierarchy (see "Universal hierarchy" earlier in this introduction), which means that men controlled society beginning with the individual family. In fact, the family metaphorically corresponded to the state. For example, the husband was the king of his family. His authority to control his family was absolute and based on divine right, similar to that of the country's king. People also saw the family itself differently than today, considering apprentices and servants part of the whole family.

The practice of *primogeniture* — a system of inheritance that passed all of a family's wealth through the first male child — accompanied this system of patriarchy. Thus women did not generally inherit their family's wealth and titles. In the absence of a male heir, some women, such as Queen Elizabeth, did. But after women married, they lost almost all of their already limited legal rights, such as the right to inherit, to own property, and to sign contracts. In all likelihood, Elizabeth I would have lost much of her power and authority if she had married.

Furthermore, women did not generally receive an education and could not enter certain professions, including acting. Instead, society relegated women to the domestic sphere of the home.

There are only three females in *Henry IV, Part 1*: Mistress Quickly, Lady Mortimer, and Lady Percy. (Each would, of course, originally have been played by a young male actor in Elizabethan times.) Mistress Quickly is one of the low-life characters, the hostess of a tavern. Her customers are happy to banter and flirt with her, but they treat her with little respect. Falstaff, indeed, speaks of her as though she were a prostitute. Lady Mortimer and Lady Percy may be nobly born, but they are firmly excluded from the decision-making of their husbands. In Lady Mortimer's case, this is emphasized by the fact that she can speak only Welsh, which her husband cannot understand. Her father, Owen Glendower, has to translate what she says to him, but when he is not there, they communicate by loving looks. She offers comfort and affection, but cannot possibly offer advice. Lady Percy is much more spirited, but Hotspur, her husband, refuses to let her know of his plans even though he acknowledges her trustworthiness: "constant you are, / but yet a woman."

Daily life

Daily life in Early Modern England began before sunup — exactly how early depended on one's station in life. A servant's responsibilities usually included preparing the house for the day. Families usually possessed limited living space, and even among wealthy families multiple family members tended to share a small number of rooms, suggesting that privacy may not have been important or practical.

Working through the morning, Elizabethans usually had lunch about noon. This midday meal was the primary meal of the day, much like dinner is for modern families. The workday usually ended around sundown or 5 p.m., depending on the season. Before an early bedtime, Elizabethans usually ate a light repast and then settled in for a couple of hours of reading (if the family members were literate and could bear the high cost of books) or socializing.

Mortality rates

Mortality rates in Early Modern England were high compared to our standards, especially among infants. Infection and disease ran rampant because physicians did not realize the need for antiseptics and sterile equipment. As a result, communicable diseases often spread very rapidly in cities, particularly London.

In addition, the bubonic plague frequently ravaged England, with two major outbreaks — from 1592–1594 and in 1603 — occurring during Shakespeare's lifetime. People did not understand the plague and generally perceived it as God's punishment. (We now know that the plague was spread by fleas and could not be spread directly from human to human.) Without a cure or an understanding of what transmitted the disease, physicians could do nothing to stop the thousands of deaths that resulted from each outbreak. These outbreaks had a direct effect on Shakespeare's career, because the government often closed the theatres in an effort to impede the spread of the disease.

London life

In the sixteenth century, London, though small compared to modern cities, was the largest city of Europe, with a population of about 200,000 inhabitants in the city and surrounding suburbs. London was a crowded city without a sewer system, which facilitated epidemics such as the plague. In addition, crime rates were high in the city due to inefficient law enforcement and the lack of street lighting.

Despite these drawbacks, London was the cultural, political, and social heart of England. As the home of the monarch and most of England's trade, London was a bustling metropolis. Not surprisingly, a young Shakespeare moved to London to begin his professional career.

The theatre

Most theatres were not actually located within the city of London. Rather, theatre owners built them on the South bank of the Thames River (in Southwark) across from the city in order to avoid the strict regulations that applied within the city's walls. These restrictions stemmed from a mistrust of public

performances as locations of plague and riotous behavior. Furthermore, because theatre performances took place during the day, they took laborers away from their jobs. Opposition to the theatres also came from Puritans who believed that they fostered immorality. Therefore, theatres moved out of the city, to areas near other sites of restricted activities, such as dog fighting, bear- and bull-baiting, and prostitution.

Despite the move, the theatre was not free from censorship or regulation. In fact, a branch of the government known as the Office of the Revels attempted to ensure that plays did not present politically or socially sensitive material. Prior to each performance, the Master of the Revels would read a complete text of each play, cutting out offending sections or, in some cases, not approving the play for public performance.

Performance spaces

Theatres in Early Modern England were quite different from our modern facilities. They were usually open-air, relying heavily on natural light and good weather. The rectangular stage extended out into an area that people called the *pit* — a circular, uncovered area about 70 feet in diameter. Audience members had two choices when purchasing admission to a theatre. Admission to the pit, where the lower classes (or *groundlings*) stood for the performances,

The recently reconstructed Globe Theatre.
Chris Parker/PAL

was the cheaper option. People of wealth could purchase a seat in one of the three covered tiers of seats that ringed the pit. At full capacity, a public theatre in Early Modern England could hold between 2,000 and 3,000 people.

The stage, which projected into the pit and was raised about five feet above it, had a covered portion called the *heavens*. The heavens enclosed theatrical equipment for lowering and raising actors to and from the stage. A trapdoor in the middle of the stage provided theatrical graves for characters such as Ophelia and also allowed ghosts, such as Banquo in *Macbeth*, to rise from the earth. A wall covered with a curtain (known as the *arras*) separated the back of the stage from the actors' dressing room, known as the *tiring house*. (In Act II, Scene 4, of *Henry IV, Part 1*, the Prince calls upon Falstaff to conceal himself from the Sheriff by hiding "behind the arras.") At each end of the wall stood a door for major entrances and exits. Above the wall and doors stood a gallery directly above the stage, reserved for the wealthiest spectators. Actors occasionally used this area when a performance called for a difference in height — for example, to represent Juliet's balcony or the walls of a besieged city. A good example of this type of theatre was the original Globe Theatre in London in which Shakespeare's company, The Lord Chamberlain's Men (later the King's Men), staged its plays. However, indoor theatres, such as the Blackfriars, differed slightly because the pit was filled with chairs

that faced a rectangular stage. Because only the wealthy could afford the cost of admission, the public generally considered these theatres private.

Actors and staging

Performances in Shakespeare's England do not appear to have employed scenery. However, theatre companies developed their costumes with great care and expense. In fact, a playing company's costumes were its most valuable items. These extravagant costumes were the object of much controversy because some aristocrats feared that the actors could use them to disguise their social status on the streets of London.

Costumes also disguised a player's gender. All actors on the stage during Shakespeare's lifetime were men. Young boys whose voices had not reached maturity played female parts. This practice no doubt influenced Shakespeare's and his contemporary playwrights' thematic explorations of cross-dressing.

Shakespeare in Love *shows how the interior of the Globe would have appeared.*
Everett Collection

Though historians have managed to reconstruct the appearance of the early modern theatre, such as the recent construction of the Globe in London, much of the information regarding how plays were performed during this era has been lost. Scholars of Early Modern theatre have turned to the scant external and internal stage directions in manuscripts in an effort to find these answers. Indeed, even the division of the text of Shakespeare's plays into scenes is often a matter of later editorial convention, and sometimes dispute. The last act of *Henry IV, Part 1*, contains five scenes, but because the action is continuous, this has no significance in performance. The text used for this edition includes many stage directions and indications of location that are traditionally accepted but have been deduced from the words said by the characters. Although a hindrance for modern critics and scholars, the lack of detail about Early Modern performances has allowed modern directors and actors a great deal of flexibility and room to be creative.

The printing press

If not for the printing press, many Early Modern plays may not have survived until today. In Shakespeare's time, printers produced all books by *sheet* — a single large piece of paper that the printer would fold in order to produce the desired book size. For example, a folio required folding the sheet once, a quarto four times, an octavo eight, and so on. Sheets would be printed one side at a time; thus, printers had to simultaneously print multiple nonconsecutive pages.

In order to estimate what section of the text would be on each page, the printer would *cast off* copy. After the printer made these estimates, *compositors* would set the type upside down, letter by letter. This process of setting type produced textual errors, some of which a proofreader would catch. When a proofreader found an error, the compositors

would fix the piece or pieces of type. Printers called corrections made after printing began *stop-press* corrections because they literally had to stop the press to fix the error. Because of the high cost of paper, printers would still sell the sheets printed before they made the correction.

Printers placed frames of text in the bed of the printing press and used them to imprint the paper. They then folded and grouped the sheets of paper into gatherings, after which the pages were ready for sale. The buyer had the option of getting the new play bound.

The printing process was crucial to the preservation of Shakespeare's works, but the printing of drama in Early Modern England was not a standardized practice. Many of the first editions of Shakespeare's plays appear in quarto format and, until recently, scholars regarded them as "corrupt." In fact, scholars still debate how close a relationship exists between what appeared on the stage in the sixteenth and seventeenth centuries and what appears on the printed page. The inconsistent and scant appearance of stage directions, for example, makes it difficult to determine how close this relationship was.

We know that the practice of the theatre allowed the alteration of plays by a variety of hands other than the author's, further complicating any efforts to extract what a playwright wrote and what was changed by either the players, the printers, or the government censors. Theatre was a collaborative environment. Rather than lament our inability to determine authorship and what exactly Shakespeare wrote, we should work to understand this collaborative nature and learn from it.

Shakespeare wrote his plays for the stage, and the existing published texts reflect the collaborative nature of the theatre as well as the unavoidable changes made during the printing process. A play's first written version would have been the author's *foul papers*, which invariably consisted of blotted lines and revised text. From there, a scribe would recopy the play and produce a *fair copy*. The theatre manager would then copy out and annotate this copy into a playbook (what people today call a *promptbook*).

At this point, scrolls of individual parts were copied out for actors to memorize. (Due to the high cost of paper, theatre companies could not afford to provide their actors with a complete copy of the play.) The government required the company to send the playbook to the Master of the Revels, the government official who would make any necessary changes or mark any passages considered unacceptable for performance.

Printers could have used any one of these copies to print a play. We cannot determine whether a printer used the author's version, the modified theatrical version, the censored version, or a combination when printing a given play. Refer back to the "Publications" section of the Introduction to William Shakespeare for further discussion of the impact printing practices has on our understanding of Shakespeare's works.

Works cited

For more information regarding Early Modern England, consult the following works:

Bevington, David. "General Introduction." *The Complete Works of William Shakespeare*. Updated Fourth edition. New York: Longman, 1997.

Greenblatt, Stephen. "Shakespeare's World." *Norton Shakespeare*. New York: W.W. Norton and Co., 1997.

Kastan, David Scott, ed. *A Companion to Shakespeare*. Oxford: Blackwell, 1999.

McDonald, Russ. *The Bedford Companion to Shakespeare: An Introduction with Documents*. Boston: Bedford-St. Martin's Press, 1996.

INTRODUCTION TO *KING HENRY IV, PART 1*

King Henry IV, Part 1 has always been one of Shakespeare's most well-loved plays. It was probably first performed in 1597, when Shakespeare's company is thought to have been working in several playhouses, including the Curtain and the Swan. Quarto editions of the play were printed in 1598 (twice), 1599, 1604, 1608, 1613, and 1622. The First Folio edition, upon which this text is based, was published in 1623. Further quartos appeared in 1632 and 1639. This large number of early printings is evidence that the play was frequently acted and that it was certainly a commercial success. It has been popular ever since.

Much of this popularity can be attributed to the fact that the play contains one of Shakespeare's most enduring comic creations, Falstaff. The earliest title page calls the play:

THE
HISTORY OF
HENRIE THE
FOVRTH;
With the battell at Shrewsburie,
between the King and Lord
Henry Percy, surnamed
Henrie Hotspur of
the North.
With the humorous conceits of Sir
Iohn Fastalffe.

Falstaff gets a mention; Prince Hal, who is really the play's hero, does not. From his first invention, Falstaff was a crowd-puller, and Shakespeare put him into *The Merry Wives of Windsor* as well as *King Henry IV, Part 2*. Referring to Falstaff on the title page was the equivalent of advertising a modern play or show by putting the name of one of its starring actors in lights. And Shakespeare drew the character of Falstaff so impressively that he has taken life beyond the plays that contained him. The nineteenth century Italian composer Verdi wrote a much-loved opera about Falstaff, with his name for its title; and the word "Falstaffian" (meaning "fat, jolly, and dissolute") is now to be found in the English dictionary.

Shakespeare's history plays

Although *Henry IV, Part 1* contains important and attractive elements of comedy, it is concerned with much more serious matters, too. It is a history play, one of a series Shakespeare wrote (including *Richard II*; *Henry IV, Part 1*; *Henry IV, Part 2*, and *Henry V*) and which together make up a *tetralogy* (from the Greek word "tetra," meaning "four"). To appreciate *Henry IV, Part 1* properly, one needs to understand what is meant by the term "history play" when we use it in reference to Shakespeare. Many of Shakespeare's plays deal with historical events, but not all of them are classified as "histories." *Antony and Cleopatra* and *Macbeth*, for example, are numbered among the tragedies, because, although they deal with true stories from the past, their real interest is in the tragic downfall of the great characters at the center of the events, not in informing the audience of historical facts, which Shakespeare readily changes or embellishes to suit his purpose.

But Shakespeare takes such liberties in his history plays, too. What unites them is not a respect for accuracy, but a common subject that is reflected in their titles: kingship.

Shakespeare's sources and how he uses them

The principle source for the main plot of *Henry IV, Part 1* was probably the second edition of Raphael Holinshed's *Chronicles* (published in 1587), but there were many other ways in which the history of the troubled reign of King Henry were known to Shakespeare and his contemporaries. Shakespeare knew and used several works that chronicled those times, including Samuel Daniel's *The Civil War Between the Two Houses of Lancaster and Yorke*, Edward Hall's *The Union of the two noble and illustre families of Lancaster and Yorke*, and Stowe's *Annals* as well as other plays including *The Famous Victories of Henry The Fifth*, a rambling and anonymous work. There was also an oral tradition including ballads and tales that kept alive the story of Henry's struggle to keep the crown he had taken. One of the most significant ways in which Shakespeare manipulates his sources is in making Hotspur and Hal the same age, when in reality many years separated them. The historical Hotspur was born before Hal's father. Knowing that Shakespeare manipulated the ages of these two characters is a clear indication that he intended them to contrast with each other in the play. He also alters the time scale of historical events to suit his purposes. *Henry IV, Part 1* begins by portraying events that took place in 1400, and ends with the Battle of Shrewsbury, which was fought in 1403. There is no sense of such time passing in the play. Shakespeare condenses history to achieve pace and urgency, as well as maintain interest.

Some of the characters and events are pure invention, of course, particularly the tavern scenes and the people that appear in them. Shakespeare took a germ of reality into his imagination and transformed it into something of his own. The character of Falstaff, one of his finest, was suggested by the real-life Sir John Oldcastle (and that was the fictional character's name, too, in the earliest draft of the play). But the real Sir John Oldcastle was nothing like Shakespeare's character, except that according to Foxe's *Acts and Monuments* (1563) he confessed at his trial for heresy that as a youth he had been given to "Pride, Wrathe, and Glottony, . . . Covetousnes and . . . Lechery" before he was condemned to a martyr's death for his religious beliefs.

Outline of the tetralogy: The context of *Henry IV, Part 1*

In order to understand and appreciate Shakespeare's purpose in *Henry IV, Part 1*, it is helpful to see how it fits in with the other three plays that together make up Shakespeare's story of the kingdom from the reign of King Richard II to the reign of King Henry V. This is not to say that the play cannot be appreciated by itself, of course; only that taking a brief look at it in its broader context makes it easier to see what Shakespeare is trying to achieve.

The problem at the heart of the tetralogy is the problem of kingship. If a king is a king because God made him one, as Elizabethans believed, what is to be done if he is a bad king? In *Richard II*, Shakespeare shows us a king who is unquestionably legitimate, but who is weak and ill-suited to the job. At the end of the play, he is deposed by Bolingbroke, who takes the throne as Henry IV. Richard is presented as an inadequate but rightful king. The sympathy of the audience is split. However, the audience is also shown how Richard is the author of his own destruction. When he seizes the property of John of Gaunt, the rightful inheritance of Bolingbroke, he acts against the very hereditary principle by which he and all monarchs reign. And the language he uses when he gives up the throne also suggests that he is acting against the will of God by abandoning his duty: He effectively "un-consecrates" himself, in a speech that is pitiful but almost blasphemous.

In *Henry IV, Part 1*, we see the consequence of this breakdown of order. Chaos and bloodshed follow it, as surely as night follows day. The main plot of the play is the story of the growing rebellion against the king who has usurped the throne. But as the rebellion grows in strength, so does Henry grow in kingly stature. And the more the rebels rebel, the more disunited they become. They rapidly descend into infighting, and a victory for them would seem to promise chaos. The way out of this opposition of two tainted causes is through the virtue of Henry's

son, Prince Hal. It is his bravery and sense of duty that significantly contribute to the defeat of the rebels at the Battle of Shrewsbury, and in the last play in the series, *Henry V*, he becomes the legendary warrior-king whose heroic virtues finally make up for the sin his father committed in deposing Richard. The price he pays is to give up the easy-going life of good-natured merry-making he enjoys with Falstaff and his friends of the tavern. Through his self-sacrifice, the Prince achieves not only personal redemption but he helps to achieve a victory of peace and stability for the kingdom as a whole. Although *Henry IV, Part 1* is indeed about the events in the first part of that king's reign, its real dramatic center is the developing character of that king's son, Prince Hal. This play, and the tetralogy as a whole, could, some suggest, be called "The Making of Henry V."

The plot of *Henry IV, Part 1*

King Henry wants peace for the kingdom, and in order to bind his people together he proposes a crusade, a campaign of holy war against the infidels who occupy the holy sites of Christianity in the Middle East. This plan has to be shelved because of news of a defeat and a victory at home. The rebellious Welsh, under Owen Glendower, have defeated the forces of Edward Mortimer, Earl of March, which had been sent to subdue them. Against the rebellious Scots, though, the King's forces, led by Harry Hotspur (the son of the Earl of Northumberland), have won a great victory. But the King is angry because Hotspur has refused to hand over any of the captives he has taken, except one. The King summons Hotspur to account for himself.

Meanwhile, the King's son and heir, Prince Hal, has been spending his time not in affairs of state but in taverns, leading a dissolute life in the company of wasters, a group dominated by Sir John Falstaff. One of this group, Ned Poins, proposes they should together rob some travelers on the Canterbury road, and they all agree upon it; but Poins' real plan is that he and the Prince should hang back, let the others commit the robbery, and then, heavily disguised, rob the robbers themselves. This is what takes place, and there is much amusement afterward, when Falstaff tells a fantastic version of the events to justify himself. By this time, though, the audience already knows that Prince Hal is determined to become a reformed character and take his responsibilities seriously. After the laughter of the robbery trick, the Prince is summoned to account for himself to his father, and Hal and Hotspur act out a dry run of the encounter to prepare the Prince for it.

When Hotspur appears before the King, he justifies his refusal to hand over the hostages to him by explaining that the King's messenger had approached him while he was exhausted from the fierce battle, and the messenger's fancy talk and dress annoyed him. Hotspur insists that he is loyal, but he still refuses to hand over the rebels for ransom, because the King has refused to buy back the Earl of Mortimer, who had been captured after his defeat by the Welsh. Mortimer is Hotspur's brother-in-law. Hotspur's uncle, the Earl of Worcester, suggests that it would be a good idea to free all his captives, and so win the support of the powerful Douglas family in the growingopposition to the King. Hotspur agrees. When the rebels meet in Wales, it is clear that Hotspur and Owen Glendower don't get along. Nevertheless, they are able to agree upon how the kingdom will be divided after they have defeated the King, at a battle planned to take place at Shrewsbury.

At the meeting between the King and Prince Hal, the King rebukes the Prince for his wayward ways, but the Prince promises to mend them and offer loyal support against the growing forces of rebellion. King Henry promises him a chance to prove himself by putting him at the head of an army. Back at the tavern, the banter is interrupted by the arrival of the Prince, who gives Falstaff a commission in the army.

Falstaff abuses this privilege by pressing into service men who are wealthy enough to pay him to buy themselves out again. The result is that the troops he ends up with are pitifully inadequate.

As the forces gather for the battle, Hotspur is told that his father is ill and can't be there, but that he advises him to carry on without him. Worse, Owen Glendower and his men are still a fortnight's march away, and Worcester's cavalry has not yet arrived. The rebels are at a disadvantage. The King mercifully offers peace to the rebels if they lay down their arms, but Worcester refuses to pass on his offer. The battle takes place, and the King's forces win. Falstaff escapes by

King Henry, as portrayed in a modern production.
Everett Collection

pretending to be dead; Hotspur is killed by Hal. The play ends, but there are other rebels yet to be beaten.

Key themes in the play

Kingship is a key theme, not just of this play, but of the tetralogy of which *Henry IV, Part 1* forms a part, and of Shakespeare's history plays in general. Another important (and related) idea that Shakespeare examines in this play is honor, and the associated notions of courage, duty, responsibility, and loyalty. These interrelated

A modern production of King Henry IV, Part 1.
Everett Collection

themes are explored through the actions of almost all of the characters in the play, high and low. The dramatic climax of the play is the courageous man-to-man struggle between two warriors, Hotspur and Hal. Each is motivated by his own view of what honor demands of him; each is loyally defending the rights of his family. Although Hal seems at first to have little care for his duties and responsibilities, he ultimately comes to be the embodiment of each. Their struggle, of course, exemplifies another of Shakespeare's recurrent interests: the conflict between order and disorder.

As in so many of Shakespeare's plays, in *Henry IV, Part 1*, he examines the difference between appearance and reality: Things in this life are often not what they seem. Hal hides his nobler qualities, for example, and Falstaff pretends to be dead when he is alive. The play also focuses on another theme that Shakespeare explores in many other places: the

relationship between parents and children (here, between the King and Prince Hal, and Northumberland and Hotspur). The King's initial disappointment by his son's irresponsible addiction to revelry is underlined by the scene in which Falstaff and Hal act out the confrontation between father and son. As the play develops, the King and the Prince become closer. Hotspur and his father, though, are separated at the end, because Northumberland's untimely illness prevents him from taking part in the battle in which Hotspur is killed.

There is a sense in which this is also a morality play (a tale showing how God punishes the evil and rewards the good). Such plays were popular for generations before Shakespeare. In morality plays, a representative of mankind has to choose between the right and the wrong way to lead his life. Morality plays included one-sided characters personifying virtues and vices that compete for the soul of man. Falstaff is very much like several of the vices rolled into one, but he is unlike any of them in that he is essentially an attractive character. It is Prince Hal who, like "Everyman," has to choose between good and evil, and whose choice is an example to us all.

Shakespeare's use of language: Poetry and prose in *Henry IV, Part 1*

Shakespeare was not just a great playwright, but a great poet, too, and a proper response to any of his plays takes this into account. Shakespeare chooses each word with a poet's care. It is important to appreciate not just *what* the characters say, but *how* they say it. The metaphors or similes they use and the images they put into our imagination work to affect the way we judge characters and events. By using images cumulatively, Shakespeare softens our subconscious so that we are in the frame of mind he intentionally creates. For example, in *Henry IV, Part 1*, Shakespeare uses repeated images of bloodshed and war alongside references to what were then thought of as unnatural events, like meteors and comets. The irresistible suggestion is that the kingdom is suffering because the natural order has been upset. A quite different example would be the endless comic variations on the way in which Falstaff's fatness is described. At the end of the play, our imaginations have been crammed with so many word-pictures of Falstaff's appearance that he seems bigger than any costume-padding could represent.

The use of imagery like this may be poetic, but it is not confined to poetry. Much of the text of this play is written in prose. Shakespeare sometimes puts prose into his characters' mouths to indicate that they are low-born, or crude, and sometimes he gives it to grander characters, to show them at ease and informal. When Prince Hal is enjoying himself with his tavern companions, he speaks with them in prose. When he is at his most princely, he speaks in verse. But most often, Shakespeare's characters speak in verse, a form of elevated speech that can convey a character's nobility or the intensity of his emotions.

In order to appreciate this play properly, it is necessary to understand the way that Shakespeare uses these two contrasting styles. The "Commentary" section of these notes explains this in more detail.

The verse Shakespeare uses is blank verse, unrhymed iambic pentameters. These terms may seem foreign and complicated, but the idea is easy enough to understand. An *iambus* is a unit of poetry (referred to as a "foot"), which is made up of two syllables — an unstressed followed by a stressed, like the word "to*day*." A pentameter is a line made up of five of these feet, so the rhythm of a typical line of Shakespearean verse would run: te-*tum* | te-*tum* | te-*tum* | te-*tum* | te-*tum*. The conventional way of marking meters is to mark a small x over unstressed syllables, and mark a forward-slash over stressed syllables, with each foot separated by a vertical line: x / | x / | x / | x / | x / . The first line of *Henry IV, Part 1* can serve as an example:

$$x \quad / \mid x \quad / \mid x \quad / \mid x \quad / \mid x \quad /$$

So sha | -ken as | we are, | so wan | with care.

Such verse is not meant to be read with a jerky "te-tum, te-tum" emphasis, of course. The rhythmic pattern should be below the surface. Blank verse is unrhymed, but Shakespeare tends to use rhymed pairs of lines (called *couplets*) to mark the ending of a scene — a useful device in Elizabethan times, because there was no curtain at the front of his stage to signify the end of a scene.

Characters in the play

One of the reasons that Shakespeare is such a great writer is that he creates characters that show that he has a deep understanding of and sympathy for the human condition. He tends to show us a character, lead us to form a judgment, and then show us something that makes us realize we have judged too easily or too harshly. Life is a complicated business, and we judge each other at our peril. Falstaff *is* an attractive rogue, whose wit and sense of fun in friendship make us admire him, and it is indeed comic to see how his clever instincts preserve him even in the serious world of war; but we are not allowed to overlook that the cost of his selfishness is the deaths of the men he sends unprepared into battle. Hotspur *is* rude, impetuous, and immature; but he dies nobly, and the Prince acknowledges his virtues at length.

Shakespeare allows us to look at different sides of the characters he creates by providing a number of parallels and contrasts. He distorts history to make Hotspur and Prince Hal the same age, so that we cannot avoid comparing one with the other. Many other such parallels can be found in the play: the relationships Hal and Hotspur have with their fathers; the relationships of Hotspur and Mortimer with their respective wives; the egotism of Glendower and Hotspur that takes shape in very different ways; the courage of the Prince when he faces Hotspur, compared with Falstaff's fear of Hotspur even when he is dead. A critical appreciation of the main characters and how they are contrasted is developed more fully in the "Commentary" section of this edition. Meanwhile, the following brief notes, along with the "Character Web" in this book, are intended to help the reader understand the role of each character and how they relate to each other.

CHARACTERS IN THE PLAY

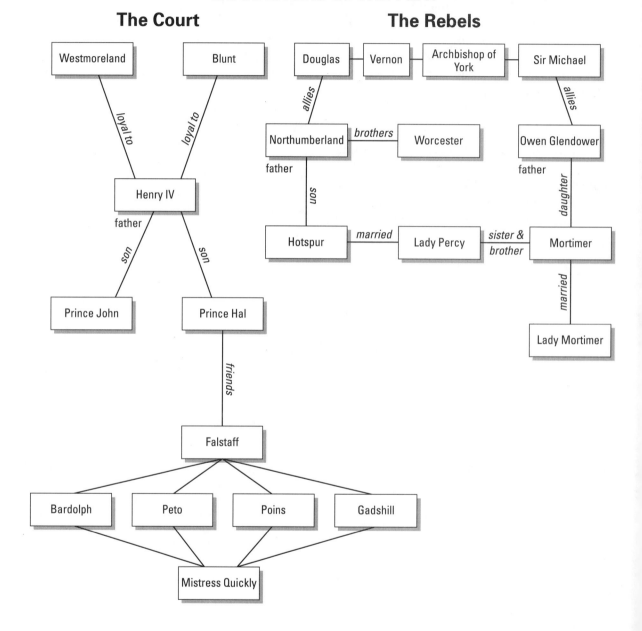

The Court

Westmoreland

Blunt

loyal to

loyal to

Henry IV

father

son

son

Prince John

Prince Hal

friends

Falstaff

Bardolph

Peto

Poins

Gadshill

Mistress Quickly

The Rebels

Douglas

Vernon

Archbishop of York

Sir Michael

allies

allies

Northumberland

brothers

Worcester

Owen Glendower

father

father

son

daughter

Hotspur

married

Lady Percy

sister & brother

Mortimer

married

Lady Mortimer

KING HENRY IV, PART 1
ACT I

Prince *And like bright metal on a sullen ground.*
My reformation, glittering o'er my fault,
Shall show more goodly and attract more eyes
Than that which hath no foil to set it off.
I'll so offend, to make offence a skill,
Redeeming time when men think least I will.

Act I, Scene 1

King Henry complains of the unsettled state of his kingdom and receives news of rebellions in Scotland and Wales. He praises the courage of Hotspur, but sends for him to account for his apparent disobedience.

ACT I, SCENE 1
London, the palace.

[*Enter* KING HENRY, LORD JOHN OF LANCASTER, THE EARL OF WESTMORELAND, SIR WALTER BLUNT, *and* Others.]

King So shaken as we are, so wan with care,
Find we a time for frighted peace to pant,
And breathe short-winded accents of new broils
To be commenced in stronds afar remote.
No more the thirsty entrance of this soil   5
Shall daub her lips with her own children's blood;
No more shall trenching war channel her fields,
Nor bruise her flowerets with the armed hoofs
Of hostile paces: those opposed eyes,
Which, like the meteors of a troubled heaven,   10
All of one nature, of one substance bred,
Did lately meet in the intestine shock
And furious close of civil butchery
Shall now, in mutual well-beseeming ranks,
March all one way and be no more opposed   15
Against acquaintance, kindred and allies:
The edge of war, like an ill sheathed knife,
No more shall cut his master. Therefore, friends,
As far as to the sepulchre of Christ,
Whose soldier now, under whose blessed cross   20
We are impressed and engaged to fight,
Forthwith a power of English shall we levy;
To chase these pagans in those holy fields
Over whose acres walk'd those blessed feet
Which fourteen hundred years ago were nail'd   25
For our advantage on the bitter cross.
But this our purpose now is twelve months old,
And bootless 'tis to tell you we will go:
Therefore we meet not now. Then let me hear
Of you, my gentle cousin Westmoreland,   30

NOTES

1. *we:* kings traditionally use the first person plural forms ("we," "us," "our") and not the singular ("I," "me," "my"). It suggests that they speak for and embody their whole kingdom.

2. *peace to pant:* metaphor (personification) expressing breathlessness of a peace that has been frightened away; relate to "breathe short-winded accents" in line 3.

3. *broils:* conflicts.

4. *stronds:* strands, shores.

8. *flowerets:* young men in the flower of their manhood.

9. *hostile paces:* enemy footsteps (hoofs indicates horses' paces).

10. *meteors:* traditionally regarded as signs of impending disaster.

12. *intestine:* internal; refers to domestic or internecine strife (suggests belly blows).

13. *close:* grappling struggle.

14. *mutual well-beseeming ranks:* more fittingly marching together against a common external foe than marching against one another.

17–18. *edge of war . . . cut his master:* a metaphor and a simile to express the damage civil war does to all sides involved.

19. *sepulchre:* tomb in the Holy Land in which Christ's body was laid prior to the resurrection. Crusaders sought to return it to Christian keeping.

21. *impressed:* pressed into (service) or conscripted.

22. *power:* army.

    levy: raise.

23. *pagans:* Saracens here, though they were not pagan in the strict sense of the term, but Mohammedan.

28. *bootless:* pointless.

What yesternight our council did decree
In forwarding this dear expedience.

Westmoreland My liege, this haste was hot in question,
And many limits of the charge set down
But yesternight: when all athwart there came   35
A post from Wales loaden with heavy news;
Whose worst was, that the noble Mortimer,
Leading the men of Herefordshire to fight
Against the irregular and wild Glendower,
Was by the rude hands of that Welshman taken,   40
A thousand of his people butchered;
Upon whose dead corpse there was such misuse,
Such beastly shameless transformation,
By those Welshwomen done as may not be
Without much shame retold or spoken of.   45

King It seems then that the tidings of this broil
Brake off our business for the Holy Land.

Westmoreland This match'd with other did, my
     gracious lord;
For more uneven and unwelcome news
Came from the north and thus it did import: 50
On Holy rood day, the gallant Hotspur there,
Young Harry Percy and brave Archibald,
That ever valiant and approved Scot,
At Holmedon met,
Where they did spend a sad and bloody hour;   55
As by discharge of their artillery,
And shape of likelihood, the news was told;
For he that brought them, in the very heat
And pride of their contention did take horse,
Uncertain of the issue any way.   60

King Here is a dear, a true industrious friend,
Sir Walter Blunt, new lighted from his horse,
Stained with the variation of each soil
Betwixt that Holmedon and this seat of ours;
And he hath brought us smooth and welcome news.   65
The Earl of Douglas is discomfited:
Ten thousand bold Scots, two and twenty knights,
Balk'd in their own blood did Sir Walter see
On Holmedon's plains. Of prisoners, Hotspur took

32.   *expedience:* expedition hastily undertaken.

35.   *but:* only.

      athwart: contrary to.

36.   *post:* messenger.

39.   *irregular:* not following the rules of war.

40.   *rude:* rough and uncivilized.

42.   *corpse:* corpses.

43.   *transformation:* Welsh women were accused of castrating the English corpses.

48.   *This matched . . . did:* This unfortunate news accompanied by other bad tidings caused the Crusade to have been postponed.

51.   *Holy-rood day:* September 14, the day on which the discovery of Christ's cross (or "rood") is commemorated.

54.   *Holmedon:* place near the Scots border.

59.   *contention:* rival claim and struggle.

64.   *seat:* home, headquarters; in this case, palace.

66.   *discomfited:* defeated (literally put out of his comfort).

68.   *Balk'd:* piled up in balks or ridges.

Mordake the Earl of Fife, and eldest son   70
To beaten Douglas; and the Earl of Athol,
Of Murray, Angus, and Menteith.
And is not this an honourable spoil?
A gallant prize? ha, cousin, is it not?

Westmoreland In faith,   75
It is a conquest for a prince to boast of.

King Yea, there thou makest me sad and makest
    me sin
In envy that my Lord Northumberland
Should be the father to so blest a son,
A son who is the theme of honour's tongue;   80
Amongst a grove, the very straightest plant;
Who is sweet Fortune's minion and her pride:
Whilst I, by looking on the praise of him,
See riot and dishonour stain the brow
Of my young Harry. O that it could be proved   85
That some night tripping fairy had exchanged
In cradle clothes our children where they lay,
And called mine Percy, his Plantagenet!
Then would I have his Harry, and he mine.
But let him from my thoughts. What think you, coz,   90
Of this young Percy's pride? the prisoners,
Which he in this adventure hath surprised,
To his own use he keeps; and sends me word,
I shall have none but Mordake Earl of Fife.

Westmoreland This is his uncle's teaching: this is   95
    Worcester,
Malevolent to you in all aspects;
Which makes him prune himself, and bristle up
The crest of youth against your dignity.

King But I have sent for him to answer this;
And for this cause awhile we must neglect   100
Our holy purpose to Jerusalem.
Cousin, on Wednesday next our council we
Will hold at Windsor, so inform the lords:
But come yourself with speed to us again;
For more is to be said and to be done   105
Than out of anger can be uttered.

Westmoreland I will, my liege. [*Exeunt.*]

---

73. *spoil:* prize won in battle.

80. *the theme of honour's tongue:* spoken of as being honorable.

82. *minion:* darling (favorite).

84. *riot:* wild living.

86. *night-tripping fairy:* Henry wishes that a fairy had exchanged his son for Percy's (Northumberland's) when they were babes in their cradles.

88. *Plantagenet:* the family name of the royal house of Anjou (France) to which Henry IV belonged.

90. *coz:* affectionate abbreviation for cousin.

97. *prune:* preen

98. *crest:* i.e., of a bird; the plume on a helmet is also suggested.

COMMENTARY

The mood is solemn; the King is troubled. His plans for a crusade to the Holy Land have to be put off because there has been so much civil unrest. Rebellions have arisen in the north, in Scotland, and in the west, in Wales. The Welsh, under the wild leadership of Owen Glendower, have savagely defeated the troops that were sent to subdue them. The Scots, however, have been beaten; but the commander of the victorious English army, Henry Percy, known as Hotspur, has refused to hand over most of his captives to the King.

Even so, King Henry admires Hotspur for his courage and honor, qualities he wishes were displayed by his own son and heir, Henry, Prince of Wales (known as Prince Hal), who has a reputation for loose living and irresponsibility. Shakespeare twists history to make Hal and Hotspur the same age, so that their characters can be closely contrasted throughout the play. (The historical Hotspur was born in 1364, three years before Hal's father was born. The real Prince Hal was born in 1387.)

Hotspur's defiance of the King is explained by Westmoreland, King Henry's loyal and level headed adviser: Hotspur is under the influence, it seems, of his uncle, the Earl of Worcester, who hates King Henry. Worcester is summoned to account for himself.

Shakespeare first portrays Henry IV as a responsible monarch who wants peace for his kingdom and who is much troubled not only by the difficulties

A Crusader, so called because of the cross they wore on their shields and surcoats. Biblioteca Civica, Padua, Italy/SuperStock

he has in achieving it now, but also by thoughts of what will happen when his ill-disciplined son inherits the throne. Henry IV's enthusiasm for the crusade shows a sense of duty to God, as well as to his subjects, although it also suggests that he would welcome the chance to take his mind off the problems he has at home by heading for the Holy Land. These problems faced by Henry IV in his homeland, and how they are resolved, are to be the subject of the play.

The broom plant, the "planta genista," which gave the name "Plantagenet" to the Angevin dynasty from which Henry was descended. Its founder, Geoffrey IV, Count of Anjou, had always worn a sprig of broom in his cap.

Shakespeare mentions three other major characters (Hal, Hotspur, and Glendower), but does not yet bring them into the play. Although it is up to the audience to form opinions of these three men, Shakespeare affects the way the audience judges them by adding many references to honor, loyalty, bravery, and duty through the imagery of the first few speeches of this opening scene.

The play has begun in verse, in formal, elevated language, which reflects the dignity and rank of characters at court and the weightiness of the matters they discuss.

Act I, Scene 2

The Prince and his friends at the tavern plan a robbery. He reveals that, beneath his fun-loving exterior, he is concealing a serious and responsible character that he will later reveal.

ACT I, SCENE 2
London, an apartment of the Prince's.

[*Enter* THE PRINCE OF WALES *and* FALSTAFF.]

Falstaff Now, Hal, what time of day is it, lad?

Prince Thou art so fat witted, with drinking of old sack and unbuttoning thee after supper and sleeping upon benches after noon, that thou hast forgotten to demand that truly which thou wouldst truly know. 5
What a devil hast thou to do with the time of day. Unless hours were cups of sack and minutes capons, and the blessed sun himself a fair wench in flame-colour'd taffeta, I see no reason why thou should'st be so superfluous to demand the time of day. 10

Falstaff Indeed you come near me now, Hal; for we that take purses go by the moon and the seven stars, and not by Phoebus, he 'that wandering knight so fair.' And, I prithee, sweet wag, when thou art king, as, God save thy grace, — majesty I should say, 15
for grace thou, wilt have none, —

Prince What, none?

Falstaff No, by my troth, not so much as will serve to be prologue to an egg and butter.

Prince Well, how then? come, roundly, roundly. 20

Falstaff Marry, then, sweet wag, when thou art king, let not us that are squires of the night's body be called thieves of the day's beauty: let us be Diana's foresters, gentlemen of the shade, minions of the moon; and let men say we be men of good gov- 25
ernment, being governed, as the sea is, by our noble and chaste mistress the moon, tinder whose counte-nance we steal.

NOTES

3.   *sack:* white wine from Spain and the Canary Islands.

7.   *capons:* specially fattened and castrated male chicken.

9.   *taffeta:* lustrous kind of silk.

11.   *you come near me:* you come close to scoring a point.

12.   *the seven stars:* the cluster of stars known as the Pleiades.

13.   *Phoebus:* Greek name for the sun.

14.   *wag:* witty fellow.

15.   *grace:* a pun; a royal or ducal title, gracefulness in the human sense, the grace of God, and the prayer before eating, which is the "prologue" to a meal.

21.   *Marry:* the lightest of oaths; by (the Virgin) Mary.

22.   *squires of the night's body:* a euphemism for highway-robbers.

23.   *Diana:* goddess of the moon and of hunting.

27.   *chaste mistress:* oxymoron; pun on "chased."

Prince Thou sayest well, and it holds well too; for
the fortune of us that are the moon's men doth ebb   30
and flow like the sea, being governed, as the sea is,
by the moon. As, for proof, now: a purse of gold most
resolutely snatched on Monday night and most disso-
lutely spent on Tuesday morning; got with swearing
'Lay by' and spent with crying 'Bring in'; now in as   35
low an ebb as the foot of the ladder and by and by
in as high a flow as the ridge of the gallows.

Falstaff By the Lord, thou sayest true, lad. And is
not my hostess of the tavern a most sweet wench.

Prince As the honey of Hybla, my old lad of the   40
castle. And is not a buff jerkin a most sweet robe of
durance?

Falstaff How now, how now, mad wag! what, in
thy quips and thy quiddities? what a plague have I
to do with a buff jerkin?   45

Prince Why, what a plague have I to do with my
hostess of the tavern?

Falstaff Well, thou hast called her to a reckoning
many a time and oft.

Prince Did I ever call for thee to pay thy part?   50

Falstaff No; I'll give thee thy due, thou hast paid
all there.

Prince Yea, and elsewhere, so far as my coin would
stretch; and where it would not, I have used my   55
credit.

Falstaff Yea, and so used it that, were it not here
apparent that thou art heir apparent — But, I prithee, sweet wag, shall there be gallows standing in
England when thou art king? and resolution thus
fobbed as it is with the rusty curb of old father   60
antic the law? Do not thou, when thou art king,
hang a thief.

Prince No; thou shalt.

Falstaff Shall I? O rare! By the Lord, I'll be a
brave judge.   65

35. *Lay by:* the cry of the highwayman to the driver of a stagecoach: "Stand and deliver!"

Bring in: the cry of a customer making an order in a tavern.

40. *Hybla:* town in Sicily well-known for its honey.

old lad of the castle: a reference to Sir John Old-castle (the name Shakespeare originally gave to Falstaff); perhaps also a reference to a real-life Southwark brothel called "The Castle" and to inns (the devil's castles) in general.

44. *quips and thy quiddities:* smart jokes and quibbles.

what a plague: what the heck.

57. *here apparent . . . heir apparent:* an obvious pun.

60. *fobbed:* cheated.

60–61. *old father antic the law:* a personification of the law as a buffoon. "Antic" was the name of a clown in Tudor comedy.

Prince Thou judgest false already: I mean, thou
shalt have the hanging of the thieves and so become
a rare hangman.

Falstaff Well, Hal, well; and in some sort it jumps
with my humour as well as waiting in the court, I
can tell you.

Prince For obtaining of suits?

Falstaff Yea, for obtaining of suits, whereof the
hangman hath no lean wardrobe. 'Sblood, I am as
melancholy as a gib cat or a lugged bear.

Prince Or an old lion, or a lover's lute.

Falstaff Yea, or the drone of a Lincolnshire bag
pipe.

Prince What sayest thou to a hare, or the melancholy of Moor-ditch?

Falstaff Thou hast the most unsavoury similes and
are indeed the most comparative, rascalliest, sweet
young Prince. But, Hal, I prithee, trouble me no
more with vanity. I would to God thou and I knew
where a commodity of good names were to be
bought. An old lord of the council rated me the other
day in the street about you, sir, but I marked him
not; and yet he talked very wisely, but I regarded
him not; and yet he talked wisely, and in the street
too.

Prince Thou didst well; for wisdom cries out in
the streets, and no man regards it.

Falstaff O, thou hast damnable iteration and art
indeed able to corrupt a saint. Thou hast done much
harm upon me, Hal; God forgive thee for it! Before
I knew thee, Hal, I knew nothing; and now am I, if
a man should speak truly, little better than one of
the wicked. I must give over this life, and I will give
it over: by the Lord, an I do not, I am a villain; I'll
be damned for never a king's son in Christendom.

Prince Where shall we take a purse to-morrow, Jack?

70

75

80

85

90

95

100

69–70. *it jumps with my humour:* it suits my mood.

72. *suits:* lawsuits (see the pun with wardrobe).

74. *'Sblood:* an oath: by Christ's/God's blood.

86. *rated:* berated, told off.

91–92. *wisdom cries out in the streets, and no man regards it:* a biblical quotation (Proverbs 1, 20–24). The Prince caps Falstaff's reference to it.

93. *damnable iteration:* devilish habit of repeating something (and twisting its meaning).

99. *an:* if.

Falstaff 'Zounds, where thou wilt lad; I'll make
one; an I do not, call me a villain and baffle me.

Prince I see a good amendment of life in thee; 105
from praying to purse-taking.

Falstaff Why, Hal, 'tis my vocation, Hal; 'tis no sin
for a man to labour in his vocation.

[*Enter* POINS.]
Poins! Now shall we know if Gadshill have set a
match. O! if men were to be saved by merit, what 110
hole in hell were hot enough for him? This is the
most omnipotent villain that ever cried 'Stand' to a
true man.

Prince Good morrow, Ned.

Poins Good morrow, sweet Hal. What says 115
Monsieur Remorse? what says Sir John Sack and
Sugar? Jack! how agrees the devil and thee about
thy soul, that thou soldest him on Good-Friday last
for a cup of Madeira and a cold capon's leg?

Prince Sir John stands to his word, the devil shall 120
have his bargain; for he was never yet a breaker of
proverbs; he will give the devil his due.

Poins Then art thou damned for keeping thy word
with the devil.

Prince Else he had been damned for cozening the 125
devil.

Poins But, my lads, my lads, to-morrow morning
by four o'clock, early at Gadshill! there are pilgrims
going to Canterbury with rich offerings, and traders
riding to London with fat purses: I have vizards for 130
you all; you have horses for yourselves: Gadshill
lies to-night in Rochester: I have bespoke supper to-
morrow night in Eastcheap: we may do it as secure
as sleep. If you will go, I will stuff your purses full
of crowns; if you will not, tarry at home and be 135
hanged.

Falstaff Hear ye, Yedward; if I tarry at home and
go not, I'll hang you for going.

---

105. *amendment:* change of heart and turning to better behavior.

107. *vocation:* used ironically for the calling of purse-taking.

112. *Stand:* the cry of the highwayman (see line 35).

116. *Monsieur Remorse:* Poins mocks at Falstaff's melancholy.

126. *cozening:* cheating.

128. *Gadshill:* both a place (as here) and a character's name. The coincidence is confusing and is probably an error.

130. *vizards:* masks.

132. *bespoke:* ordered.

135. *crowns:* five shilling pieces.

137. *Yedward:* an affectionate, high-spirited version of Edward.

Poins You will, chops?

Falstaff Hal, wilt thou make one?   140

Prince Who, I rob? I a thief? not I, by my faith.

Falstaff There's neither honesty, manhood, nor
good fellowship in thee, nor thou camest not of the
blood royal, if thou darest not stand for ten shil-
lings.   145

Prince Well then, once in my days I'll be a madcap.

Falstaff Why, that's well said.

Prince Well, come what will, I'll tarry at home.

Falstaff By the Lord, I'll be a traitor then, when
thou art king.   150

Prince I care not.

Poins Sir John, I prithee, leave the prince and me
alone: I will lay him down such reasons for this adventure that he shall go.

Falstaff Well, God give thee the spirit of persua-   155
sion and him the ears of profiting, that what thou
speakest may move and what he hears may be believed, that the true prince may, for recreation sake,
prove a false thief; for the poor abuses of the time
want countenance. Farewell: you shall find me in   160
Eastcheap.

Prince Farewell, thou latter spring! farewell,
All-hallown summer!

[*Exit* FALSTAFF.]

Poins Now, my good sweet honey lord, ride with us
to-morrow: I have a jest to execute that I cannot   165
manage alone. Falstaff, Bardolph, Peto and
Gadshill shall rob those men that we have already
waylaid; yourself and I will not be there; and when
they have the booty, if you and I do not rob them,
cut this head off from my shoulders.   170

Prince How shall we part with them in setting
forth?

139.   *chops:* fat-face.

162.   *thou latter spring . . . All hallow summer:*
Falstaff engages in the sports of youth though he
is old. All Saints/All Hallows Day falls on
November 1, when summer weather would be
inappropriate.

167.   *Gadshill:* one of the thieves (not to be confused
with the place located between London and
Rochester, on the road to Canterbury).

Poins Why, we will set forth before or after them, and appoint them a place of meeting, wherein it is at our pleasure to fail, and then will they adventure upon the exploit themselves; which they shall have no sooner achieved, but we'll set upon them. 175

Prince Yea, but 'tis like that they will know us by our horses, by our habits and by every other appointment, to be ourselves. 180

Poins Tut! our horses they shall not see; I'll tie them in the wood; our vizards we will change after we leave them: and, sirrah, I have cases of buckram for the nonce, to immask our noted outward garments. 185

Prince Yea, but I doubt they will be too hard for us.

Poins Well, for two of them, I know them to be as true-bred cowards as ever turned back; and for the third, if he fight longer than he sees reason, I'll forswear arms. The virtue of this jest will be the incomrehensible lies that this same fat rogue will tell us when we meet at supper: how thirty, at least, he fought with; what wards, what blows, what extremities he endured; and in the reproof of this lies the jest. 190   195

Prince Well, I'll go with thee: provide us all things necessary and meet me to-morrow night in Eastcheap; there I'll sup. Farewell.

Poins Farewell, my lord. [*Exit.*]

Prince I know you all, and will awhile uphold 200
The unyoked humour of your idleness:
Yet herein will I imitate the sun,
Who doth permit the base contagious clouds
To smother up his beauty from the world,
That, when he please again to be himself, 205
Being wanted, he may be more wonder'd at,
By breaking through the foul and ugly mists
Of vapours that did seem to strangle him.
If all the year were playing holidays,
To sport would be as tedious as to work; 210

184–185. *cases of buckram for the nonce:* suits of coarse cloth for the occasion.

190. *virtue:* the essence or chief point.

191. *fat rogue:* Falstaff.

193. *wards:* defensive gestures.

198. *Eastcheap:* the market district at the north end of London Bridge.

203. *base contagious clouds:* low-flying clouds (literally earth-touching) that harbor disease.

But when they seldom come, they wish'd-for come.
And nothing pleaseth but rare accidents.
So, when this loose behaviour I throw off
And pay the debt I never promised,
By how much better than my word I am,   215
By so much shall I falsify men's hopes;
And like bright metal on a sullen ground.
My reformation, glittering o'er my fault,
Shall show more goodly and attract more eyes
Than that which hath no foil to set it off.   220
I'll so offend, to make offence a skill,
Redeeming time when men think least I will.

220. *no foil to set it off:* nothing to contrast it with.

221. *make offence a skill:* skillfully turn my misdeeds into advantages when the right time comes.

COMMENTARY

The mood changes instantly in Scene 2. In direct contrast with the opening scene of the play, the characters now speak in prose, which is informal, relaxed, and more like everyday speech. Shakespeare moves the action away from the public world of kings and courtiers talking of problems of state in grand language, and now shows us two friends joking with and teasing each other. Falstaff speaks first, addressing the Prince of Wales, eldest son of King Henry and heir to his throne, with striking intimacy. Falstaff calls him "Hal," a familiar form of the name Henry, and in the same line calls him "lad," which emphasizes Falstaff's age, the Prince's youth, and the closeness of their friendship. The Prince replies in the same vein: He teases him in a way that only a good friend would tolerate. Falstaff asks what time it is, and Hal mocks him for asking, telling Falstaff that he is such a lazy, muddle-headed, and self-indulgent eater, drinker, and womanizer that he has no need to keep track of time. The speech of each is peppered with light oaths such as "What a devil," "Marry," "By the Lord," and "what a plague." These lines emphasize the informality of their relationship and are very unprincely.

Falstaff and Prince Henry exchange jokes and banter on the subject of highway robbery, especially at night. We shall see the relevance of this later. Hal is evasive about how he will behave when he eventually becomes king, when it will be his duty to stamp out such crimes. Hal does not allow such thoughts to spoil the enjoyment of the moment, and Falstaff tells him how he is criticized for keeping low company now. Poins, another of the Prince's drinking companions, enters, and he also teases Falstaff for his faults. But when he speaks to Prince Hal, he is not as overly familiar with him as Falstaff is, and addresses him as "my lord."

Poins tells the others that he has learned that some wealthy pilgrims will be traveling to Canterbury the next day and invites them to join in robbing them. He has a plan worked out. Hal says he's not interested; Falstaff leaves, and Poins then tells the Prince his real plan: that Hal and he should play a joke upon Falstaff and the others by waiting until they have robbed the travelers and then, in disguise, stealing from them what they have stolen. Poins and the Prince know that Falstaff and his companions are cowards and braggarts, and it will be amusing to hear how they report the incident afterward. Hal agrees, and Poins exits, leaving the Prince alone on the stage.

Hal then makes one of the most important speeches of the play. It takes the form of a *soliloquy,* a conventional method of revealing a character's thoughts to the audience, whom he addresses directly. (Today's film-makers use a similar device, when they show a shot of a character's unspeaking face with a voiceover of his or her thoughts. In each case, the convention is that what the character says is what he or she is genuinely thinking.) Hal now speaks in blank verse, which reflects the seriousness of what he is saying and emphasizes that his mind is on higher things. He has been conceal-ing his real character by keeping company with all these idle tavern types. Hal says that he will be like the sun, which seems even more magnificent and desirable when it reappears from behind clouds and fogs that have temporarily obscured its beauty. When people see his own reformed character after it has been obscured by his present and past behavior, it will be all the more impressive for the contrast. The speech as a whole offers a number of variations on the idea that familiar-ity breeds contempt, or that we appreciate things the more if we have to do without them for a while. He has a strong sense of duty, and when he shows himself in his true colors, his "reformation" will be all the more impressive and men will rally to his cause. He is biding his time. The audience looks forward to the change but doesn't know when it will come.

This speech is so important partly because it under-lines an important theme of the play: the difference between appearance and reality. It also draws our attention to the moral change we are to see in the Prince: He will go through a "reformation," a term charged with religious significance that Elizabethan audiences would have been quick to pick up (see the "Religious Context" section of this edition's "Introduc-tion to Early Modern England").

Shakespeare has also started the audience's mind working along specifically moral lines by putting refer-ences to "God," "the Lord," and "Christendom" into the dialogue between Falstaff and the Prince. Their banter (beginning at line 91) about the text "wisdom cries out in the streets, and no man regards it" from the Book of Proverbs in the Bible does the same. Falstaff's response to the Prince's quotation is comic in its absurd evasion of responsibility, but it is also full of the language of Christian morality. For all the light-heartedness of the occasion, the repetition of such terms such as "corrupt as a saint," "God forgive thee," "one of the wicked," "I'll be damned," and "'tis no sin" give a moral dimension to their amusing mischief-making.

Shakespeare's introduction of Falstaff, meanwhile, is a strong one. Falstaff's larger-than-life character and appearance is emphasized not just by what he says and does, but by how each of the other characters in the scene talks about him. Poins, too, teases Falstaff for his epic self-indulgence, addressing him as "Sir John Sack and Sugar" and "Monsieur Remorse" in a probable ref-erence to an alcoholic hangover. He also reminds Fal-staff that he had jokingly sold his soul to the devil last Good Friday — the most somber day in the Christian cal-endar, when Christ's crucifixion is commemorated — for a glass of wine and a leg of chicken. This jesting not only emphasizes Falstaff's love of food but keeps up the pattern of religious diction. This language may be the language of the Morality play (see the "Introduction" section of this edition), but its tone is not as serious. Even so, the audience has been drip-fed with the ideas of the Judgment that awaits such vices, however attractive they may seem for the moment.

Act I, Scene 3

Hotspur and the other Percys appear before the King, and harsh words are exchanged. When the King leaves, they discuss their reasons for hating and mistrusting him. Worcester reveals that there is a rebellion planned against the King, and they all agree to it.

ACT I, SCENE 3
London, the palace.

[*Enter* THE KING, NORTHUMBERLAND, WORCES-
TER, HOTSPUR, SIR WALTER BLUNT, *with* Others.]

King My blood hath been too cold and temperate,
Unapt to stir at these indignities,
And you have found me; for accordingly
You tread upon my patience: but be sure
I will from henceforth rather be myself,   5
Mighty and to be fear'd, than my condition;
Which hath been smooth as oil, soft as young down,
And therefore lost that title of respect
Which the proud soul ne'er pays but to the proud.

Worcester Our house, my sovereign liege, little   10
    deserves
The scourge of greatness to be used on it;
And that same greatness too which our own hands
Have holp to make so portly.

Northumberland My lord, —

King Worcester, get thee gone; for I do see   15
Danger and disobedience in thine eye:
O, sir, your presence is too bold and peremptory,
And majesty might never yet endure
The moody frontier of a servant brow.
You have good leave to leave us: when we need   20
Your use and counsel, we shall send for you.

[*Exit* WORCESTER.]
You were about to speak. [*To* NORTHUMBERLAND.]

Northumberland   Yea, my good lord.
Those prisoners in your highness' name demanded,
Which Harry Percy here at Holmedon took,
Were, as he says, not with such strength denied   25

NOTES

2.   *Unapt:* disinclined.

3.   *found me:* i.e., found me so.

6.   *my condition:* my usual self.

10.   *Our house:* i.e., the Percies and their associates.

11.   *scourge of greatness:* i.e., the scourge (literally a whip for inflicting punishment), which those in power are able to authorize.

13.   *holp:* helped.

      portly: weighty and important.

17.   *peremptory:* stubborn.

19.   *moody frontier of a servant brow:* frowning forehead of a servant.

20.   *good leave:* full permission.

26.   *deliver'd:* reported.

As is deliver'd to your majesty:
Either envy, therefore, or misprision
Is guilty of this fault and not my son.

Hotspur My liege, I did deny no prisoners.
But I remember, when the fight was done,   30
When I was dry with rage and extreme toil,
Breathless and faint, leaning upon my sword,
Came there a certain lord, neat and trimly dress'd,
Fresh as a bridegroom; and his chin new reap'd
Show'd like stubble-land at harvest-home;   35
He was perfumed like a milliner,
And 'twixt his finger and his thumb he held
A pouncet-box, which ever and anon
He gave his nose and took't away again;
Who therewith angry, when it next came there,   40
Took it in snuff; and still he smiled and talk'd,
And as the soldiers bore dead bodies by,
He call'd them untaught knaves, unmannerly,
To bring a slovenly unhandsome corse
Betwixt the wind and his nobility.   45
With many holiday and lady terms
He question'd me; amongst the rest, demanded
My prisoners in your majesty's behalf.
I then, all smarting with my wounds being cold,
To be so pester'd with a popinjay,   50
Out of my grief and my impatience
Answer'd neglectingly I know not what,
He should, or he should not; for he made me mad
To see him shine so brisk and smell so sweet
And talk so like a waiting-gentlewoman   55
Of guns and drums and wounds — God save the
     mark —
And telling me the sovereign'st thing on earth
Was parmaceti for an inward bruise;
And that it was great pity, so it was,
This villainous salt-petre should be digg'd   60
Out of the bowels of the harmless earth,
Which many a good tall fellow had destroy'd
So cowardly; and but for these vile guns,
He would himself have been a soldier.
This bald unjointed chat of his, my lord,   65

27. *misprision:* misunderstanding or error of communication.

38. *pouncet-box:* snuff box. Relate to line 41.

44. *corse:* corpse.

45. *Betwixt:* between.

46. *holiday and lady terms:* dainty and effeminate phrases.

50. *popinjay:* a parrot or, as here, a coxcomb. Note the effect of scorn achieved by alliterating the *p* consonant.

56. *God save the mark:* the phrase here expresses indignation

58. *parmaceti:* spermaceti (obtained from whales).

60. *salt-petre:* nitre (used in explosives and medicine).

I answer'd indirectly, as I said;
And I beseech you, let not his report
Come current for an accusation
Betwixt my love and your high majesty.

Blunt The circumstance consider'd, good my lord,   70
Whate'er Lord Harry Percy then had said
To such a person and in such a place,
At such a time, with all the rest retold,
May reasonably die and never rise
To do him wrong or any way impeach   75
What then he said, so he unsay it now.

King Why, yet he doth deny his prisoners,
But with proviso and exception,
That we at our own charge shall ransom straight
His brother-in-law, the foolish Mortimer;   80
Who, on my soul, hath wilfully betray'd
The lives of those that he did lead to fight
Against that great magician, damn'd Glendower,
Whose daughter, as we hear, the Earl of March
Hath lately married. Shall our coffers, then,   85
Be emptied to redeem a traitor home?
Shall we buy treason? and indent with fears,
When they have lost and forfeited themselves?
No, on the barren mountains let him starve;
For I shall never hold that man my friend   90
Whose tongue shall ask me for one penny cost
To ransom home revolted Mortimer.

Hotspur Revolted Mortimer!
He never did fall off, my sovereign liege,
But by the chance of war; to prove that true   95
Needs no more but one tongue for all those wounds,
Those mouthed wounds, which valiantly he took,
When on the gentle Severn's sedgy bank,
In single opposition, hand to hand,
He did confound the best part of an hour   100
In changing hardiment with great Glendower:
Three times they breathed, and three times did they
    drink,
Upon agreement, of swift Severn's flood;

69. *come current for:* come rushing in as.

75. *impeach:* question in an accusatory tone.

77. *yet:* still.

78. *But:* except.

84. *Earl of March:* i.e., Mortimer.

94. *fall off:* become a rebel or traitor.

97. *mouthed:* gaping.

98. *Severn:* the River that separates England and southeast Wales.

Sedgy: bordered with reeds.

101. *changing hardiment:* exchanging hard blows.

102. *drink:* by accident (when they fell into the river). By agreement is ironic.

Who then, affrighted with their bloody looks,
Ran fearfully among the trembling reeds,　　　　　　　　105
And hid his crisp head in the hollow bank
Bloodstained with these valiant combatants.
Never did base and rotten policy
Colour her working with such deadly wounds;
Nor never could the noble Mortimer　　　　　　　　110
Receive so many, and all willingly:
Then let not him be slander'd with revolt.

King Thou dost belie him, Percy, thou dost belie
　　　him;
He never did encounter with Glendower;
I tell thee,　　　　　　　　115
He durst as well have met the devil alone
As Owen Glendower for an enemy.
Art thou not ashamed? But, sirrah, henceforth
Let me not hear you speak of Mortimer:
Send me your prisoners with the speediest means,　　　　120
Or you shall hear in such a kind from me
As will displease you. My Lord Northumberland,
We license your departure with your son.
Send us your prisoners, or you will hear of it.

[*Exeunt* KING HENRY, BLUNT, *and* Train.]

Hotspur An if the devil come and roar for them,　　　　125
I will not send them: I will after straight
And tell them so; for I will ease my heart,
Albeit I make a hazard of my head.

Northumberland What, drunk with choler? stay
　　　and pause awhile:
Here comes your uncle.　　　　　　　　130

[*Re-enter* WORCESTER.]

Hotspur　　　　　　　　Speak of Mortimer!
'Zounds, I will speak of him; and let my soul
Want mercy, if I do not join with him:
Yea, on his part I'll empty all these veins,
And shed my dear blood drop by drop in the dust,
But I will lift the down-trod Mortimer　　　　135
As high in the air as this unthankful king,

---

104. *Who then, affrighted:* the river was frightened of their wounded appearance and ran fearfully. This figure of speech is called *pathetic fallacy,* in which nature (the river) is made (by Shakespeare) capable or responding (by running fearfully) to human emotions (the fighting Mortimer and Glendower). The basic metaphor is sustained for several lines by such words as head, color, and wounds.

110. *Nor never:* a double negative, which, though ungrammatical today, was emphatic in Elizabethan usage.

113. *belie him:* tell a lie about him.

121. *such a kind:* in such a manner.

129. *choler:* blind unreasoning rage.

131. *'Zounds:* an oath; corruption of "by God's wounds."

132. *want:* lack; i.e., may I be damned.

As this ingrate and canker'd Bolingbroke.

Northumberland Brother, the king hath made your
    nephew mad.

Worcester Who struck this heat up after I was
    gone?

Hotspur He will, forsooth, have all my prisoners;   140
And when I urged the ransom once again
Of my wife's brother, then his cheek look'd pale,
And on my face he turn'd an eye of death,
Trembling even at the name of Mortimer.

Worcester I cannot blame him: was not he pro-   145
    claim'd
By Richard, that dead is, the next of blood?

Northumberland He was; I heard the proclama-
    tion:
And then it was when the unhappy king, —
Whose wrongs in us God pardon! — did set forth
Upon his Irish expedition;   150
From whence he intercepted did return
To be deposed and shortly murdered.

Worcester And for whose death we in the world's
    wide mouth
Live scandalized and foully spoken of.   155

Hotspur But soft, I pray you; did King Richard
    then
Proclaim my brother Edmund Mortimer
Heir to the crown?

Northumberland   He did; myself did hear it.

Hotspur Nay, then, I cannot blame his cousin
    king,
That wish'd him on the barren mountains starve.
But shall it be, that you, that set the crown   160
Upon the head of this forgetful man
And for his sake wear the detested blot
Of murderous subornation, shall it be,
That you a world of curses undergo,
Being the agents, or base second means,   165
The cords, the ladder, or the hangman rather?

137. *ingrate and canker'd Bolingbroke:* ungrateful and diseased. Hotspur scornfully refers to Henry by the name by which he was known before he became king.

146. *By Richard:* A reference to Richard's proclamation that Mortimer was to succeed to the throne. This happened shortly before Richard left for the Irish Rebellion during which he was forced to return to England where he was deposed, imprisoned, and shortly afterwards murdered.

155. *scandalized:* disgraced.

156. *soft:* take it easy.

157. *brother:* brother-in-law.

163. *subornation:* inciting somebody else to commit a crime; in this case, treason and regicide.

O, pardon me, that I descend so low,
To show the line and the predicament
Wherein you range under his subtle king;
Shall it for shame be spoken in these days,   170
Or fill up chronicles in days to come,
That men of your nobility and power
Did gage them both in an unjust behalf
As both of you — God pardon it! — have done,
To put down Richard, that sweet lovely rose,   175
And plant this thorn, this canker, Bolingbroke?
And shall it in more shame be further spoken,
That you are fool'd, discarded and shook off
By him for whom these shames ye underwent?
No; yet time serves wherein ye may redeem   180
Your banish'd honours and restore yourselves
Into the good thoughts of the world again,
Revenge the jeering and disdain'd contempt
Of this proud king, who studies day and night
To answer all the debt lie owes to you   185
Even with the bloody payment of your deaths:
Therefore, I say, —

Worcester   Peace, cousin, say no more:
And now I will unclasp a secret book,
And to your quick-conceiving discontents
I'll read you matter deep and dangerous,   190
As full of peril and adventurous spirit
As to o'er-walk a current roaring loud
On the unstead fast footing of a spear.

Hotspur If he fall in, good-night! or sink or swim:
Send danger from the east unto the west,   195
So honour cross it from the north to south,
And let them grapple: O, the blood more stirs
To rouse a lion than to start a bare!

Northumberland Imagination of some great exploit
Drives him beyond the bounds of patience.   200

Hotspur By heaven, methinks it were an easy leap,
To pluck bright honour from the pale-faced moon,
Or drive into the bottom of the deep,
Where fathom-line could never touch the ground,

173. *gage:* pledge.

188. *unclasp a secret book:* i.e., reveal a conspiracy.

193. *the unsteadfast footing of a spear:* by balancing on an unsteady spear.

196. *So:* so long as, provided that.

And pluck up drowned honour by the locks;   205
So he that doth redeem her thence might wear
Without corrival all her dignities:
But out upon this half-faced fellowship!

Worcester He apprehends a world of figures here,
But not the form of what he should attend.   210
Good cousin, give me audience for a while.

Hotspur I cry you mercy.

Worcester   Those same noble Scots
That are your prisoners, —

Hotspur   I'll keep them all;
By God, he shall not have a Scot of them;
No, if a Scot would save his soul, he shall not: 215
I'll keep them, by this hand.

Worcester   You start away
And lend no ear unto my purposes.
Those prisoners you shall keep.

Hotspur   Nay, I will; that's flat.
He said he would not ransom Mortimer;
Forbad my tongue to speak of Mortimer;   220
But I will find him when he lies asleep,
And in his ear I'll holla 'Mortimer!'
Nay,
I'll have a starling shall be taught to speak
Nothing but 'Mortimer', and give it him,   225
To keep his anger still in motion.

Worcester Hear you, cousin; a word.

Hotspur All studies here I solemnly defy,
Save how to gall and pinch this Bolingbroke:
And that same sword and buckler Prince of Wales,   230
But that I think his father loves him not
And would be glad he met with some mischance,
I would have him poison'd with a pot of ale.

Worcester Farewell, kinsman: I'll talk to you
When you are better temper'd to attend.   235

Northumberland Why, what a wasp-stung and impatient fool

209–210. *He apprehends . . . attend:* Worcester says that Hotspur sees with his imagination what he should do but is not capable of paying attention to the practical details that are what he ought to be attending to.

229. *gall and pinch:* irritate and annoy.

230. *sword and buckler:* insulting because these weapons were used only by serving men and men of inferior rank and fortune.

Art thou to break into this woman's mood,
Tying thine ear to no tongue but thine own!

Hotspur Why, look you, I am whipp'd and scourged
    with rods,
Nettled and stung with pismires, when I hear   240
Of this vile politician, Bolingbroke.
In Richard's time — what do you call the place? —
A plague upon it, it is in Gloucestershire,
'Twas where the madcap duke his uncle kept,
His uncle York; where I first bow'd my knee   245
Unto this king of smiles, this Bolingbroke, —
'Sblood! —
When you and he came back from Ravenspurgh.

Northumberland At Berkley castle.

Hotspur You say true: 250
Why, what a candy deal of courtesy
This fawning greyhound then did proffer me!
Look, 'when his infant fortune came to age',
And, 'gentle Harry Percy', and 'kind cousin';
O, the devil take such cozeners! God forgive me!   255
Good uncle, tell your tale; I have done.

Worcester Nay, if you have not, to it again;
We will stay your leisure.

Hotspur   I have done, i' faith.

Worcester Then once more to your Scottish pris-
    oners.
Deliver them up without their ransom straight,   260
And make the Douglas' son your only mean
For powers in Scotland; which, for divers reasons
Which I shall send you written, be assured,
Will easily be granted. You, my lord, [*To
    Northumberland*]
Your son in Scotland being thus employ'd,   265
Shall secretly into the bosom creep
Of that same noble prelate, well beloved,
The archbishop.

Hotspur Of York, is it not?

Worcester True; who bears hard   270
His brother's death at Bristol, the Lord Scroop.

---

240. *pismires:* ants.

242. *what . . . place?:* Hotspur cannot remember the name of Berkley Castle, because he is so worked up.

248. *Ravenspurgh:* the port at which Henry Bolingbroke landed on returning from exile.

251. *candy deal of courtesy:* the sweet politeness with which Henry Bolingbroke treated Hotspur and the other Percys in order to win their support. Note the originality of the phrase and the effective alliteration of the *c* consonant.

255. *cozeners:* cheaters. A pun on "kind cousin."

260. *straight:* immediately.

267. *prelate:* clergyman of high rank.

I speak not this in estimation,
As what I think might be, but what I know
Is ruminated, plotted and set down,
And only stays but to behold the face   275
Of that occasion that shall bring it on.

Hotspur I smell it: upon my life, it will do well.

Northumberland Before the game is afoot, thou
    still let'st slip.

Hotspur Why, it cannot choose but be a noble plot: 280
And then the power of Scotland and of York,
To join with Mortimer, ha?

Worcester   And so they shall.

Hotspur In faith, it is exceedingly well aim'd.

Worcester And 'tis no little reason bids us speed,
To save our heads by raising of a head.   285
For, bear ourselves as even as we can,
The king will always think him in our debt,
And think we think ourselves unsatisfied,
Till he hath found a time to pay us home:
And see already how he doth begin   290
To make us strangers to his looks of love.

Hotspur He does, he does: we'll be revenged on him.

Worcester Cousin, farewell: no further go in this
Than I by letters shall direct your course.
When time is ripe, which will be suddenly,   295
I'll steal to Glendower and Lord Mortimer;
Where you and Douglas and our powers at once,
As I will fashion it, shall happily meet,
To bear our fortunes in our own strong arms,
Which now we hold at much uncertainty.   300

Northumberland Farewell, good brother: we shall
    thrive, I trust.

Hotspur Uncle, adieu: O, let the hours be short
Till fields and blows and groans applaud our sport!
[*Exeunt.*]

285. *head:* an army.

289. *pay us home:* pay us out.

295. *suddenly:* immediately.

COMMENTARY

Scene 3 returns to blank verse: Shakespeare starts the action once more at court, to which the King has summoned the Percy clan. The King is more determined and decisive than when Shakespeare first introduced him in Act I, Scene 1. He is resolved to act like a king and take command of the events that have been troubling his realm.

Worcester speaks up for his "house," the Percys, and begins to sing its praises, but he is immediately ordered away by the King for being too haughty. Henry's words of dismissal — "You have good leave to leave us" — are a serious insult. He is determined not to tolerate challenges to his rule.

King Henry then asks Northumberland what he has to say for himself. Northumberland defends his son, Hotspur, against the charge that he had been disloyal by refusing to deliver up the Scottish prisoners to the King. Hotspur himself explains (without waiting to be asked) that he had been outraged by the offensive manner of the King's envoy, who turned up at the end of the battle in spotless fine clothes to make his demands in fancy and unmanly language, with no respect for what the warriors had been through. No wonder he answered this lord's demands "indirectly" (and no doubt angrily). This situation was reported to the King as a refusal. The language Hotspur uses to describe the messenger's manner and appearance is full of scorn. Calling him "fresh as a bridegroom" is ironically insulting. The repeated letter "p" sound in "perfumed" and "pouncet" emphasizes his contempt. (Linguists call "p" a "plosive" sound, and its explosive qualities emphasize the mood of Hotspur's speech. He almost spits out the words.) The picture of the messenger taking delicate pinches of snuff while surrounded by the dead, dying, and wounded is vivid and sickening. No wonder Hotspur reacted angrily to this tactless envoy. Sir Walter Blunt, a loyal and fair-minded supporter of the King, surely speaks for the audience when he says that it would be unfair to hold Hotspur's hot words against him, given such provocation.

But Hotspur still hasn't handed back the prisoners, says the King, who goes on to insult "foolish Mortimer," Hotspur's brother-in-law, pointing out that he not only treacherously surrendered to the King's great enemy, Owen Glendower, but married his daughter. Henry has no intention of ransoming him.

Hotspur reacts with fury to these insults to his sister's husband, who he says fought hand-to-hand with Glendower with great valor. Henry dismisses this report as a lie, demands that Hotspur hand over the prisoners, and leaves.

Hotspur is fuming, "drunk with choler," as his father puts it. He rages against the King, calling him "canker'd Bolingbroke," referring to him by his family name in a way that shows he thinks of him not as a rightful King but as a usurper. A discussion follows to remind the audience of how Henry got the throne. His predecessor, Richard II, had named Mortimer as his successor before Richard was imprisoned and murdered, leaving Bolingbroke to claim it. That, says Hotspur, is why the King hates Mortimer and calls him a traitor.

Hotspur angrily complains that the Percys have been shamed by siding with "this canker, Bolingbroke" against King Richard, "that sweet lovely rose," and are now even more disgraced by putting up with the tyranny of the man they helped make King. Worcester starts to tell Hotspur of a secret plan to overthrow Henry, but Hotspur is so carried away with anger that he hardly allows Worcester a chance to speak. Hotspur declares that he will do whatever he can to "gall and pinch this Bolingbroke" and his son, Prince Hal. Northumberland criticizes Hotspur for being too fond of the sound of his own voice, but Hotspur's anger continues; he is so worked up that he can't even remember the name of Berkeley Castle, where he first bowed his knee to King Henry. At last, Hotspur allows Worcester to speak.

Worcester is far calmer in his determination to overthrow Henry, and has thought out how it is to be done. He tells Hotspur to release the Scottish prisoners without asking for ransom, keeping back only the son of the Earl of Douglas. This will win the favor of the Scots, and keep them in touch. Worcester tells Northumberland to creep "secretly into the bosom" of the Archbishop of York, who also has reasons to hate Henry: He blames him for the death of his brother. Worcester himself will "steal to" Glendower and Mortimer, to draw them into the plot, and when the time is ripe, they will all gather together an army to overthrow the King.

Sword and buckler, late fifteenth century.

Hotspur, hot-headed as ever, instantly agrees to the plan without question. He enthusiastically looks forward to the battle, which he refers to as "sport," a word that suggests a devil-may-care attitude to matters of life and death. Just as the previous scene closes with Prince Hal showing himself to be growing in maturity and responsibility, so this scene closes with an emphatic picture of Hotspur as an impetuous youth. Shakespeare clearly intends the audience to see the contrast. Another way in which we are intended to contrast the two men is in the way that they relate to their fathers. In Act I, Scene 1, King Henry has expressed his sadness that his own eldest son is not like Hotspur; in this scene, we see how Hotspur's father is unable to control him.

Notes

Notes

KING HENRY IV, PART 1
ACT II

Lady *But hear you, my lord.*

Hotspur *What say'st thou, my lady?*

Lady *What is it carries you away?*

Hotspur *Why, my horse, my love, my horse.*

Act II, Scene 1

The Chamberlain of an inn tells Gadshill of some rich travelers who will be worth robbing.

ACT II, SCENE 1
Rochester, an inn yard.

[*Enter a* Carrier *with a lantern in his hand.*]

First Carrier Heigh-ho! an it be not four by the day I'll be hanged: Charles' wain is over the new chimney and yet our horse not packed. What, ostler!

Ostler [*Within*] Anon, anon.

First Carrier I prithee, Tom, beat Cut's saddle, put a few flocks in the point; poor jade, is wrung in the withers out of all cess.   5

[*Enter another* Carrier.]

Second Carrier Peas and beans are as dank here as a dog, and that is the next way to give poor jades the bots: this house is turned upside down since Robin   10
Ostler died.

First Carrier Poor fellow, never joyed since the price of oats rose; it was the death of him.

Second Carrier I think this be the most villainous house in all London road for fleas: I am stung like a   15
tench.

First Carrier Like a tench! by the mass, there is ne'er a king christen could be better bit than I have been since the first cock. What, Ostler! come away and be hanged! come away.   20

Second Carrier I have a gammon of bacon and two razes of ginger, to be delivered as far as charing-cross.

First Carrier God's body! the turkeys in my pannier are quite starved. What, ostler! A plague on thee!   25
hast thou never an eye in thy head? canst not hear?

NOTES

1. *carrier:* one who transports goods on pack-horses.

   an: if.

   by the day: a.m.

2. *Charles' wain:* the constellation called the Great Bear. Wain means wagon.

3. *horse:* horses.

   ostler: stable-lad.

4. *anon:* immediately, i.e., "I'm coming, I'm coming!"

5. *Cut's:* common name for a work horse.

6. *flocks:* pieces of wool for padding.

   point: sharp point of the saddle that needed padding to prevent abrasion.

   jade: sorry, "ill-conditioned" horse.

7. *wrung in the withers:* rubbed sore on the shoulder-blade.

   out of all cess: excessively.

8. *dank:* humid (damp).

9. *next:* quickest.

10. *bots:* disease of horses caused by parasitic worms or maggots.

12. *joyed:* enjoyed (his work).

16. *tench:* a fresh-water fish spotted as if covered with fleas.

18. *king christen:* Christian king.

19. *first cock:* midnight.

20. *and be hanged:* i.e., "damn you."

22. *razes:* roots.

22–23. *charing-cross:* a London landmark.

24. *pannier:* wicker side baskets slung over the horse so as to hang down on either side in a balanced position.

An't were not as good deed as drink, to break the
pate on thee I am a very villain. Come, and be
hanged! hast no faith in thee?

[*Enter* GADSHILL.]

Gadshill Good morrow, carriers. What's o'clock?   30

First Carrier I think it be two o'clock.

Gadshill I prithee, lend me thy lantern, to see my
gelding in the stable.

First Carrier Nay, by God, soft; I know a trick
worth two of that, i' faith.   35

Gadshill I pray thee, lend me thine.

Second Carrier Ay, when? canst tell? Lend me thy
lantern quoth he? marry, I'll see thee hanged first.

Gadshill Sirrah carrier, what time do you mean to
come to London?   40

Second Carrier Time enough to go to bed with a
candle, I warrant thee. Come, neighbour Mugs, we'll
call up the gentlemen: they will along with company, for they have great charge. [*Exeunt Carriers.*]

Gadshill What, ho! chamberlain.   45

Chamberlain [*Within*] At hand, quoth pick-purse.

Gadshill That's even as fair as — at hand, quoth the
chamberlain; for thou variest no more from picking
of purses than giving direction doth from labouring;
thou layest the plot how.   50

[*Enter* CHAMBERLAIN.]

Chamberlain Good morrow, Master Gadshill. It
holds current that I told you yesternight: there's a
franklin in the wild of Kent hath brought three hundred marks with him in gold: I heard him tell it to
one of his company last night at supper; a kind of   55
auditor; one that hath abundance of charge too, God
knows what. They are up already, and call for eggs
and butter: they will away presently.

27. *An't:* if it.

28. *pate:* skull.

31. *two o'clock:* (The First Carrier previously
announced it was four o'clock.)

42. *Mugs:* common name for a country bumpkin.

44. *great charge:* a lot to look after.

46. *At hand:* "Here I am!"

51. *Chamberlain:* servant in charge of rooms at an
inn.

53. *franklin:* yeoman landowner, a rank below the
gentry.

    wild: the Weald, an upland area of Kent.

54. *marks:* a mark was worth two-thirds of a pound.

56. *auditor:* official of the royal Treasury.

    charge: responsibility.

58. *presently:* at once.

Gadshill Sirrah, if they meet not with Saint Nicholas' clerks, I'll give thee this neck.   60

Chamberlain No, I'll none of it: I pray thee, keep that for the hangman; for I know thou worshippest Saint Nicholas as truly as a man of falsehood may.

Gadshill What talkest thou to me of the hangman? if I hang, I'll make a fat pair of gallows; for if I   65
hang, old Sir John hangs with me, and thou knowest he is no starveling. Tut! there are other Trojans that thou dreamest not of, the which for sport sake are content to do the profession some grace; that would, if matters should be looked into, for their own credit   70
sake, make all whole. I am joined with no foot-land rakers, no long-staff sixpenny strikers, none of these mad mustachio purple-hued malt-worms; but with nobility and tranquility, burgomasters and great-oneyers, such as can hold in, such as will strike   75
sooner than speak, and speak sooner than drink, and drink sooner than pray; and yet 'zounds, I lie, for they pray continually to their saint, the commonwealth; or rather, not pray to her, but prey on her, for they ride up and down on her and make her their   80
boots.

Chamberlain What, the commonwealth their boots? will she hold out water in foul way?

Gadshill She will, she will; justice hath liquored her. We steal as in a castle, cock-sure; we have the   85
receipt of fern-seed, we walk invisible.

Chamberlain Nay, by my faith, I think you are more beholding to the night than to fern-seed for your walking invisible.

Gadshill Give me thy hand: thou shalt have a share   90
in our purchase, as I am a true man.

Chamberlain Nay, rather let me have it, as you are a false thief.

Gadshill Go to; 'homo' is a common name to all men. Bid the ostler bring my gelding out of the   95
stable. Farewell, you muddy knave. [*Exeunt.*]

59–60. *St. Nicholas:* patron saint of robbers.

clerks: euphemism for highwaymen.

64. *What:* why.

67. *Trojans:* epic name used satirically for heroes.

71–72. *foot-land rakers:* wandering footpads (thieves).

72. *long-staff sixpenny strikers:* thieves bearing long staffs, who are willing to knock down a victim for the sake of a small reward (sixpence).

73. *purple-hued malt-worm:* purplefaced beer-drinkers.

75. *oneyers:* Nobody is certain what this word means; "honeyers" has been suggested to mean smooth talkers. Others take it for a legal term meaning "a sheriff accountable to the king for monies due."

81. *boots:* booty (reward). A pun.

83. *foul way:* when the roads were bad (as, in the sixteenth century, they usually were, especially after rain).

84–85. *justice hath liquored her:* the poor manner in which justice is enforced makes crime (especially highway robbery) common in the state (commonwealth); to "liquor" boots was to make them waterproof.

86. *fern-seed:* a plant popularly believed to make persons invisible.

91. *purchase:* plunder.

94. *homo:* the generic name for man (homo sapiens).

96. *muddy:* muddle-headed.

COMMENTARY

Act II includes a dramatic change of tone and mood that holds the audience's interest and returns to the comic subplot of the trick that the Prince and Poins have prepared for Falstaff and his companions.

A franklin.
The Huntington Library, Art Collections, and Botanical Gardens, San Marino, California/SuperStock

Shakespeare suddenly takes the play far from the cares of state and grand affairs of politics and treason. Two *carriers*, the Tudor equivalent of long-distance truck drivers, arrive at an inn-yard in the middle of the night. (One carries a lantern, the conventional way of representing darkness in an age when the stage was lit by daylight.) Their language is in marked contrast to that of the previous scene. Act I, Scene 3, was full of ideas, its speeches marked by abstract nouns: "greatness," "honour," "shame," and the like. The world of the carriers and ostlers is littered with peas, beans, dogs, horses, and fleas. It is a world full of things and low creatures, not notions. The diction that Shakespeare uses conveys a sense of the harsh realities of everyday life.

Gadshill arrives and asks the carriers to lend him their lantern so he can see his way to stable his horse. They refuse because they don't trust him — and their instinct is correct. Gadshill has come to speak to the inn's Chamberlain, who has told him that there are some guests worth robbing. The Chamberlain confirms that this is the case, and Gadshill asserts that he will rob them, and boasts that he will escape the hangman.

This situation is an example of "dramatic irony:" The audience knows something that Gadshill doesn't. He is about to be tricked, and he will, in turn, be robbed himself. He confidently sets off to meet his friends and commit the crime, but we know that there is a surprise in store for them.

Act II, Scene 2

Falstaff, Gadshill, Bardolph, and Peto rob the travelers; the Prince and Poins, disguised, rob the robbers.

ACT II, SCENE 2
The highway, near Gadshill.

[*Enter* PRINCE HENRY *and* POINS.]

Poins Come, shelter, shelter: I have removed Falstaff's horse, and he frets like a gummed velvet.

Prince Stand close.

[*Enter* FALSTAFF.]

Falstaff Poins! Poins, and be hanged! Poins!

Prince Peace, ye fat-kidneyed rascal! what a braw-   5
ling dost thou keep!

Falstaff Where's Poins, Hal?

Prince He is walked up to the top of the hill: I'll
go seek him.

Falstaff I am accursed to rob in that thief's com-   10
pany: the rascal hath removed my horse, and tied
him I know not where. If I travel four foot by the
squier further afoot I shall break my wind. Well, I
doubt not but to die a fair death for all this, if I I
'scape hanging for killing that rogue. I have forsworn   15
his company hourly any time this two and twenty
years, and yet I am bewitched with the rogue's company. If the rascal have not given me medicines to
make me love him, I'll be hanged; it could not be
else; I have drunk medicines. Poins! Hal! a plague   20
upon you both! Bardolph! Peto! I'll starve ere I'll
rob a foot further. An 'twere not as good a deed as
drink, to turn true man and to leave these rogues, I
am the veriest varlet that ever chewed with a tooth.
Eight yards of uneven ground is threescore and ten   25
miles afoot with me; and the stony-hearted villains
know it well enough: a plague upon it when thieves
cannot be true to one another! [*They whistle.*]

NOTES

2. *frets:* a play on two meanings of this word: (1) is
vexed, (2) frays or wears and fears easily.

4. *and be hanged:* damn you.

13. *squier:* carpenter's set square.

14. *doubt not but to:* expect I will.

18. *medicines:* love potions.

22. *An:* if.

24. *varlet:* servant.

Whew! A plague upon you all! Give me my horse, you rogues; give me my horse, and be hanged. 30

Prince Peace! lie down; lay thine ear close to the ground and list if thou canst hear the tread of travellers.

Falstaff Have you any levers to lift me up again, being down? 'Sblood, I'll not bear mine own flesh so 35 far afoot again for all the coin in thy father's exchequer. What a plague mean ye to colt me thus.

Prince Thou liest; thou art not colted, thou art uncolted.

Falstaff I prithee, good Prince Hal, help me to my 40 horse, good king's son.

Prince Out, ye rogue! shall I be your ostler?

Falstaff Go, hang thyself in thine own heir-apparent garters. If I be ta'en, I'll peach for this. An I have not ballads made on you all and sung to filthy tunes, 45 let a cup of sack be my poison: when a jest is so forward, and afoot too! I hate it.

[*Enter GADSHILL, BARDOLPH and PETO with him*]

Gadshill Stand.

Falstaff So I do, against my will.

Poins O, 'tis our setter, I know his voice. Bardolph, 50 what news?

Bardolph Case ye, case ye; on with your vizards: there's money of the king's coming down the hill; 'tis going to the king's exchequer.

Falstaff You lie, you rogue; tis going to the king's 55 tavern.

Gadshill There is enough to make us all.

Falstaff To be hanged.

Prince Sirs, you four shall front them in the narrow lane; Ned Poins and I will walk lower: if they 'scape 60 from your encounter, then they light on us.

Peto How many be there of them?

37. *colt:* make a fool of or deceive.

38. *uncolted:* unhorsed (or dehorsed).

42. *shall I . . .:* Prince Hal rebuffs Falstaff's request. He is not Sir John's servant!

43. *heir-apparent:* next in line to the throne.

44. *garters:* pun on Order of the Garter, which is an order of chivalry.

     peach: inform on.

45. *ballads:* satirical verses set to music for singing in the streets.

50. *setter:* criminal who sets up the crime.

52. *Case ye:* mask yourselves.

     vizards: masks.

54. *king's exchequer:* the royal treasury.

59. *front:* confront or face.

61. *light:* alight upon.

Gadshill Some eight or ten.

Falstaff Zounds, will they not rob us?

Prince What, a coward, Sir John Paunch?   65

Falstaff Indeed, I am not John of Gaunt, your
grandfather, but yet no coward, Hal.

Prince Well, we leave that to the proof.

Poins Sirrah Jack, thy horse stands behind the
hedge: when thou needest him, there thou shalt find   70
him. Farewell, and stand fast.

Falstaff Now cannot I strike him, if I should be
hanged.

Prince Ned, where are our disguises.

Poins Here, hard by: stand close.   75

[*Exeunt* PRINCE *and* POINS.]

Falstaff Now, my masters, happy man be his dole,
say I: every man to his business.

[*Enter the* Travellers.]

First Traveller Come, neighbor: the boy shall lead
our horses down the hill; we'll walk afoot awhile,
and ease our legs.   80

Thieves Stand!

Travellers Jesus bless us!

Falstaff Strike; down with them; cut the villains'
throats: ah! caterpillars! bacon-fed knaves! they
hate us youth: down with them: fleece them.   85

Travellers O, we are undone, both we and ours for-
ever!

Falstaff Hang ye, knaves, are ye undone? No, ye
fat chuffs; I would your store were here! On, bacons,
on! What, ye knaves! young men must live. You are   90
grandjurors, are ye? we'll jure ye, 'faith.

[*Here they rob them and bind them. Exeunt.*]

[*Re-enter* PRINCE HENRY *and* POINS.]

66.   *Gaunt:* the English form of Ghent (where Hal's grandfather, John o'Gaunt, came from). Note the pun on gaunt (meaning lean) and Paunch (meaning fat belly) on line 65.

76.   *happy man be his dole:* may every man be dealt out a portion of the reward from this robbery.

85.   *youth:* the collective plural comically includes old Falstaff.

91.   *grandjurors:* owning enough property to be eligible to sit on a grand jury; men of substance.

Prince The thieves have bound the true men. Now
could thou and I rob the thieves and go merrily to
London, it would be argument for a week, laughter
for a month and a good jest for ever.   95

Poins Stand close; I hear them coming.

[*Enter the* Thieves *again*.]

Falstaff Come, my masters, let us share, and then to
horse before day. An the Prince and Poins be not
two arrant cowards, there's no equity stirring: there's
no more valour in that Poins than in a wild-duck.   100

Prince Your money!

Poins Villains!

[*As they are sharing, the* PRINCE *and* POINS *set upon them;
they all run away; and* FALSTAFF, *after a blow or two, runs
away too, leaving the booty behind them*.]

Prince Got with much ease. Now merrily to horse.
The thieves are all scatter'd and possess'd with fear
So strongly that they dare not meet each other;   105
Each takes his fellow for an officer.
Away, good Ned. Falstaff sweats to death,
And lards the lean earth as he walks along.
Were't not for laughing, I should pity him.

Poins How the rogue roar'd! [*Exeunt*.]   110

99.   *equity:* fair play.

106.   *officer:* officer of the watch, the equivalent of
police.

108.   *lards the lean earth:* perspires into and thus
greases the soil.

COMMENTARY

The robbery plot quickly unfolds. Poins has stolen Falstaff's horse, forcing him to travel on foot. Falstaff is so fat and unfit that he can hardly walk any distance at all, and his loud protests comically underline the absurd figure that he cuts as he struggles along in the company of the Prince. He moans about Poins's treachery: "a plague on it when thieves cannot be true to one another." This scene is another example of dramatic irony, for Falstaff makes the remark to Hal, who we know is also about to deceive Falstaff. Falstaff's remark about Poins is also a reference to the idea of loyalty, one of the key themes of the play.

Bardolph, Peto, and Gadshill arrive. (Gadshill is also the name of the place at which the robbery happens. The confusing choice of names may be a mistake or a miscopying of Shakespeare's original words.) Their victims are coming down the hill. The Prince tells the three men to go ahead with Falstaff while he and Poins hang back. (The audience knows the reason for Hal and Poins separating from the others — another example of dramatic irony.) When it is revealed that the robbers are outnumbered by their victims, Falstaff immediately expresses fear: "Zounds, will they not rob us?", but when it comes time to execute the robbery, he at least bombards them with terrifying and blood-curdling language. Falstaff is clearly a man of talk rather than action, unless that action is eating, drinking, or making merry.

Bardolph, Peto, and Gadshill tie up their victims and while they are sharing out the booty, Falstaff complains of the cowardice of Poins and the Prince in not taking part in the robbery. In another example of dramatic irony, Falstaff says that "there's no more valour in that Poins than in a wild duck" the very moment before Poins and the Prince, disguised, set upon their friends and steal from them what they have stolen. As the robbed robbers run off, the Prince describes their panic, and we are left with the mental picture of Falstaff sweating so much as he flees that he "lards the lean earth."

Falstaff, Gadshill, Bardolph, and Peto do not, of course, know who has set upon them, and the audience

The Badge of the order of the Garter, the highest English Order of Chivalry. The main part of its insignia is a richly decorated garter, worn on the thigh.

knows that, when they meet up with Poins and the Prince, they will have to explain what has happened. Their excuses will be the best part of the joke.

This scene is a highly successful comic one, but amidst all the laughter, it also operates at a much more serious level. On the one hand, the scene celebrates the friendship between the tavern companions, including the Prince. Practical jokes rarely work well unless they are practiced by friends upon friends. This joke is a big one, suggesting big friendship. On the other hand, this is a joke that depends upon betrayal; and betrayal and loyalty are important themes in this play. The scene is funny and good-natured; but it is also a variation on a theme that is played out much more tragically in the main plot of the play, the story of the rebellion against the King.

Act II, Scene 3

Hotspur reads a letter advising the rebels to delay. His wife, Kate, asks him what is on his mind, because he has been talking of war in his sleep. He refuses to tell her.

ACT II, SCENE 3
Warkworth Castle.

[*Enter* HOTSPUR, *solus, reading a letter.*]

Hotspur "*But, for mine own part, my lord, I could be well contented to be there, in respect of the love I bear your house.*" He could be contented: why is he not, then? In respect of the love he bears our house: he shows in this, he loves his own barn better than he loves our house. Let me see some more. "*The purpose you undertake is dangerous;*" — why, that's certain: 'tis dangerous to take a cold, to sleep, to drink; but I tell you, my lord fool, out of this nettle, danger, we pluck this flower, safety. "*The purpose you undertake is dangerous; the friends you have named uncertain; the time itself unsorted; and your whole plot too light for the counterpoise of so great an opposition.*" Say you so, say you so? I say unto you again, you are a shallow cowardly hind, and you lie. What a lack-brain is this! By the Lord, our plot is a good plot as ever was laid; our friends true and constant: a good plot, good friends, and full of expectation; an excellent plot, very good friends. What a frosty-spirited rogue is this! Why, my lord of York commends the plot and the general course of the action. 'Zounds, an I were now by this rascal, I could brain him with his lady's fan. Is there not my father, my uncle and myself? lord Edmund Mortimer, my lord of York and Owen Glendower? is there not besides the Douglas? have I not all their letters to meet me in arms by the ninth of the next month? and are they not some of them set forward already? What a pagan rascal is this! an infidel! Ha! you shall see

NOTES

5

10

15

20

25

8.   *take:* catch.

12.   *unsorted:* ill-chosen.

13.   *counterpoise:* weight used to balance against another weight of equivalent heaviness.

15.   *hind:* servant.

29.   *pagan . . . infidel:* a topical reference during the period of the Crusades. This reference makes him sound like a Saracen (one who did not share his faith).

now in very sincerity of fear and cold heart, will he   30
to the king and lay open all our proceedings. O, I
could divide myself and go to buffets, for moving
such a dish of skim milk with so honourable an action! Hang him! let him tell the king: we are prepared. I will set forward to-night.   35

[*Enter* LADY PERCY.]
How now, Kate! I must leave you within these two
　　hours.

Lady O, my good lord, why are you thus alone?
Tell me, sweet lord, what is't that takes from thee
Thy stomach, pleasure and thy golden sleep?
Why dost thou bend thine eyes upon the earth,   40
And start so often when thou sitt'st alone?
Why hast thou lost the fresh blood in thy cheeks;
And given my treasures and my rights of thee
To thick-eyed musing and cursed melancholy?
In thy faint slumbers I by thee have watch'd,   45
And heard thee murmur tales of iron wars;
Speak terms of manage to thy bounding steed;
Cry 'Courage! to the field!' And thou hast talk'd
Of sallies and retires, of trenches, tents,
Of palisadoes, frontiers, parapets,   50
Of basilisks, of cannon, culverin,
Of prisoners' ransom and of soldiers slain,
And all the currents of a heady fight.
Thy spirit within thee hath been so at war
And thus hath so bestirr'd thee in thy sleep,   55
That beads of sweat have stood upon thy brow
Like bubbles in a late-disturbed stream;
And in thy face strange motions have appear'd,
Such as we see when men restrain their breath
On some great sudden best. O, what portents are   60
　　these?
Some heavy business hath my lord in hand,
And I must know it, else he loves me not.

Hotspur What, ho!
[*Enter* Servant.]
　　　　　Is Gilliams with the packet gone?

Servant He is, my lord, an hour ago.

30.　*will he:* he will go.

32.　*buffets:* fight myself.

43.　*my rights of thee:* her conjugal rights of Hotspur.

47.　*manage:* direction and management of a battle.

49.　*sallies:* advances.

　　　retires: retreats.

50.　*palisadoes:* rows of stakes placed for defensive reasons.

　　　frontiers: barriers.

　　　parapets: walls.

51.　*basilisks:* heavy gun.

　　　culverin: long thin rifle.

60.　*hest:* behest.

　　　portents: signs or omens.

Hotspur Hath Butler brought those horses from the   65
    sheriff?

Servant One horse, my lord, he brought even now.

Hotspur What horse? a roan, a crop-ear, is it not?

Servant It is, my lord.

Hotspur   That roan shall be my throne.
    Well, I will back him straight: O Esperance!
    Bid Butler lead him forth into the park. [*Exit Servant.*]   70

Lady But hear you, my lord.

Hotspur What say'st thou, my lady?

Lady What is it carries you away?

Hotspur Why, my horse, my love, my horse.

Lady Out, you mad-headed ape!   75
    A weasel hath not such a deal of spleen
    As you are toss'd with. In faith,
    I'll know your business, Harry, that I will.
    I fear my brother Mortimer doth stir
    About his title, and hath sent for you   80
    To line his enterprise: but if you go, —

Hotspur So far afoot, I shall be weary, love.

Lady Come, come, you paraquito, answer me
    Directly unto this question that I ask:
    In faith, I'll break thy little finger, Harry,   85
    An if thou wilt not tell me all things true.

Hotspur Away,
    Away, you trifler! Love! I love thee not,
    I care not for thee, Kate: this is no world
    To play with mammets and to tilt with lips: 90
    We must have bloody noses and crack'd crowns,
    And pass them current too. God's me, my horse!
    What say'st thou, Kate? what wouldst thou have
        with me?

Lady Do you not love me? do you not, indeed?
    Well, do not then; for since you love me not,   95
    I will not love myself. Do you not love me?
    Nay, tell me if you speak in jest or no.

---

67. *roan:* reddish horse flecked with white.

69. *back him:* get on his back, mount.

Esperance: "hope" (French). The family motto of the Percys was "Esperance ma conforte" (meaning "Hope (is) my comfort").

76. *spleen:* fiery impetuosity.

80. *title:* claim to the throne based on Richard II's expressed wish.

81. *line:* assist and support.

83. *paraquito:* parrot.

90. *mammets:* dolls or puppets.

tilt: kiss passionately (the image of taking opposite sides in a tournament and encountering one another violently).

91. *crowns:* heads/coins.

92. *pass them current:* accept them as good currency.

Hotspur Come, wilt thou see me ride?
　And when I am o' horseback, I will swear
　I love thee infinitely. But hark you, Kate,　　　　　　100
　I must not have you henceforth question me
　Whither I go, nor reason whereabout:
　Whither I must, I must; and, to conclude,
　This evening must I leave you, gentle Kate.
　I know you wise, but yet no farther wise　　　　　　105
　Than Harry Percy's wife: constant you are,
　But yet a woman: and for secrecy,
　No lady closer; for I well believe
　Thou wilt not utter what thou dost not know;
　And so far will I trust thee, gentle Kate.　　　　　　110

Lady How! so far?

Hotspur Not an inch further. But hark you, Kate:
　Whither I go, thither shall you go too;
　To-day will I set forth, to-morrow you.
　Will this content you, Kate?　　　　　　115

Lady　　　　　　　　　　　　It must of force. [*Exeunt.*]

108.　　*No lady closer:* none more able to keep a secret.

COMMENTARY

In Act II, Scene 3, the play returns to its main plot: the developing rebellion against King Henry. Shakespeare forces the audience to wait a while to see the outcome of the jest that has been played upon Falstaff. Running the two stories in tandem like this is a clever way of keeping up the pace and interest of the play. Only later will the two strands of the tale intertwine. Now the action goes to the Percy castle at Warkworth. Warkworth was (and still is) a huge and dominant complex of buildings reflecting the power and influence the Percys then enjoyed in the north of England.

The atmosphere is instantly conspiratorial. Hotspur is alone, reading a letter by an unnamed author, which adds to the sense of secrecy and subterfuge. Hotspur reads parts of it aloud. It is sympathetic to the rebel cause, but its author refuses to join them at that time for several good reasons, not least of which is that they are not yet strong enough to stand a chance of winning. Hotspur dismisses each argument in turn, showing himself to be more interested in action than caution. He

reacts to the advice with contempt and angrily accuses the author of cowardice. Hotspur's language reflects his fiery loss of temper. He condemns the letter-writer as a "fool," a "shallow, cowardly hind," a "lack-brain," a "frosty-spirited rogue," a "rascal," a "pagan rascal," and an "infidel." He assumes that the writer of the letter will betray the rebels to the King. But this doesn't matter: Hotspur is setting off to join the other rebels that very evening.

The audience quickly sees Hotspur's reaction to the letter as an indication of the way in which his temper gets the better of his judgment. He will not listen to advice. To emphasize this point, we now see how he refuses to allow his own wife into his confidence, although we must remember that this would be less of a shock to Shakespeare's contemporaries than it is to us. (See the "Introduction to Early Modern England" section of this book.) Kate, Lady Percy, is distressed to be given only two hours' notice that her husband is to leave. She knows that something is happening, because

Warkworth Castle today.
SuperStock

Hotspur has been behaving strangely recently, becoming melancholy and introspective. Moreover, he has been talking in his sleep about weapons, battles, and death. What is on his mind? Hotspur doesn't even answer her, but calls for a servant and orders him to saddle his new horse so that he can try it out.

Hotspur's wife is furious that he won't reveal his plans to her, because she loves him and is frightened for him. She has guessed what is going on, though he doesn't admit it. Kate also knows his weakness: "A weasel has not such a deal of spleen / As you are tossed with." They quarrel, but it is clear that they love each other. Even so, he refuses to tell her of his plans. For all her constancy, she is a woman, and women, he suggests, cannot be trusted with secrets. Hotspur will, however, allow Kate to follow him, though he won't yet tell her where.

In this intimate little scene, Shakespeare shows Hotspur close up, leaving the audience with an even stronger impression of Hotspur's impetuosity, for this quality even comes between Hotspur and his wife. But Kate loves him in spite of it, and that fact makes us feel that he must have a sympathetic side, too. We wonder what the outcome of the battle will be. On the one hand, we know that Hotspur is outwardly confident; but we also now know that he is subconsciously worried. The measured prose of the letter suggests that the writer has weighed the odds before deciding that the chances are against the rebels succeeding, and the audience is left to wonder whether Hotspur has been right to dismiss its advice so readily. Once again, Shakespeare ends the scene leaving the audience anxious to discover what will happen next.

Act II, Scene 4

The Prince has some fun at the tavern, first by teasing a foolish young servant, and then by listening to Falstaff's dishonest account of the robbery. When the trick is revealed, Falstaff laughs it off. Falstaff and the Prince act out the upcoming confrontation between the Prince and his father. Falstaff falls asleep when hiding from the Sheriff, and the Prince picks his pockets.

ACT II, SCENE 4
The Boar's-head Tavern, Eastcheap.

[*Enter the* PRINCE *and* POINS.]

Prince Ned, prithee, come out of that fat room, and
  lend me thy hand to laugh a little.

Poins Where hast been, Hal?

Prince With three or four loggerheads amongst
  three or four score hogsheads. I have sounded the   5
  very base-string of humility. Sirrah, I am sworn
  brother to a leash of drawers; and can call them all
  by their christen names, as Tom, Dick, and Francis.
  They take it already upon their salvation, that though
  I be but Prince of Wales, yet I am the king of cour-   10
  tesy; and tell me flatly I am no proud Jack, like Falstaff, but a Corinthian, a lad of mettle, a good boy,
  by the Lord, so they call me, and when I am king of
  England I shall command all the good lads in Eastcheap. They call drinking deep, dyeing scarlet; and   15
  when you breathe in your watering, they cry 'hem!'
  and bid you play it off. To conclude, I am so good a
  proficient in one quarter of an hour, that I can drink
  with any tinker in his own language during my life.
  I tell thee, Ned, thou hast lost much honour, that thou   20
  wert not with me in this action. But, sweet Ned, — to
  sweeten which name of Ned, I give thee this pennyworth of sugar, clapped even now into my hand by
  an under-skinker, one that never spoke other English
  in his life than 'Eight shillings and sixpence', and   25
  'You are welcome', with this shrill addition, 'Anon,
  anon, sir! Score a pint of bastard in the Half-moon',
  or so. But, Ned, to drive away the time till Falstaff
  come, I prithee do thou stand in some by-room, while

NOTES

1.   *fat:* probably "vat."

4.   *loggerheads:* numbskulls.

5.   *hogsheads:* largest-sized barrels made by the coopers.

7.   *leash:* collective noun taken from a pack of hounds on the leash.

    drawers: ale-servers, tapsters.

12.   *Corinthian:* a pleasure-loving fellow (from the city of Corinth, which was notorious for its "pleasure").

    mettle: courage.

16.   *breathe in your watering:* probably means to take breath when you drink; the idea is to finish the glass (of beer) without taking a breath.

18.   *proficient:* this adjective is here used as a noun; it is not so employed today.

24.   *under-skinker:* under-drawer.

26.   *anon:* at once.

27.   *bastard:* wine of common or undetermined origin.

    Half-moon: name of a room in the tavern.

I question my puny drawer to what end he gave me   30
the sugar; and do thou never leave calling 'Francis',
that his tale to me may be nothing but 'Anon'. Step
aside, and I'll show thee a precedent.

Poins Francis!

Prince Thou art perfect.   35

Poins Francis! [Exit POINS.]

[*Enter* FRANCIS.]

Francis Anon, anon, sir. Look down into the Pomgarnet, Ralph.

Prince Come hither, Francis.

Francis My lord?   40

Prince How long hast thou to serve, Francis?

Francis Forsooth, five years, and as much as to —

Poins [*Within*] Francis!

Francis Anon, anon, sir.

Prince Five year! by'r lady, a long lease for the   45
clinking of pewter. But, Francis, darest thou be so
valiant as to play the coward with thy indenture and
show it a fair pair of heels and run from it?

Francis O Lord, sir, I'll be sworn upon all the books
in England, I could find in my heart.   50

Poins [*Within*] Francis!

Francis Anon, sir.

Prince How old art thou, Francis?

Francis Let me see — about Michaelmas next I shall
be —   55

Poins [*Within*] Francis!

Francis Anon, sir. Pray stay a little, my lord.

Prince Nay, but hark you, Francis: for the sugar
thou gavest me, 'twas a pennyworth, was't not?

Francis O Lord, I would it had been two!   60

Prince I will give thee for it a thousand pound: ask
me when thou wilt, and thou shalt have it.

---

33.   *precedent:* example.

37.   *Pomgarnet:* Pomegranate, another named room.

41.   *to serve:* Francis' apprenticeship in serving.

45.   *by'r lady:* by Our Lady (the Virgin Mary).

47.   *indenture:* deed of apprenticeship.

49.   *books:* i.e., bibles and prayerbooks.

54.   *Michaelmas:* September 29.

Poins [*Within*] Francis!

Francis Anon, anon.

Prince Anon, Francis? No, Francis; but to-mor-　　　65
row, Francis; or Francis, o' Thursday; or indeed,
Francis, when thou wilt. But Francis!

Francis My lord?

Prince Wilt thou rob this leathern jerkin, crystal-
button, not-pated, agate-ring, puke-stocking, caddis-　　　70
garter smooth-tongue, Spanish-pouch, —

Francis O Lord, sir, who do you mean?

Prince Why then, your brown bastard is your only
drink; for look you, Francis, your white canvas doublet will sully: in Barbary, sir, it cannot come to so　　　75
much.

Francis What, sir?

Poins [*Within*] Francis!

Prince Away, you rogue! dost thou not hear them
call?　　　80

[*Here they both call him; the drawer stands amazed, not knowing which way to go.*]

[*Enter* VINTNER.]

Vintner What, standest thou still, and hearest such
a calling? Look to the guests within. [*Exit* FRANCIS.]
My lord, old Sir John, with half-a-dozen more, are at
the door: shall I let them in?

Prince Let them alone awhile, and then open the　　　85
door.

[*Exit* VINTNER.] Poins!

[*Re-enter* POINS.]

Poins Anon, anon, sir.

Prince Sirrah, Falstaff and the rest of the thieves
are at the door; shall we be merry?　　　90

Poins As merry as crickets, my lad. But hark ye;
what cunning match have you made with this jest of
the drawer? come, what's the issue?

70. *not-pated:* short-haired (a lower class style).

puke: dark wool (poor quality).

caddis: coarse tape.

71. *Spanish-pouch:* i.e., pouch of Spanish leather.

75. *Barbary:* north Africa.

81. *Vintner:* literally, one who manufactures wine, but in this case the supervisor of the serving men; a manager.

Prince I am now of all humours that have showed
themselves humours since the old days of goodman   95
Adam to the pupil age of this present twelve o'clock
at midnight. [*Re-enter* FRANCIS.] What's o'clock,
Francis?

Francis Anon, anon, sir. [*Exit.*]

Prince That ever this fellow should have fewer   100
words than a parrot, and yet the son of a woman!
His industry is up-stairs and down-stairs; his elo-
quence the parcel of a reckoning. I am not yet of
Percy's mind, the Hotspur of the north; he that kills
me some six or seven dozen of Scots at a breakfast,   105
washes his hands, and says to his wife 'Fie upon this
quiet life! I want work.' 'O my sweet Harry,' says
she, 'how many hast thou killed today?' 'Give my
roan horse a drench,' says he; and answers 'Some
fourteen,' an hour after; 'a trifle, a trifle.' I prithee,   110
call in Falstaff. I'll play Percy, and that huge brawn
shall play Dame Mortimer, his wife. 'Rivo!' says the
drunkard. Call in ribs, call in tallow.

[*Enter* FALSTAFF, GADSHILL, BARDOLPH, *and* PETO;
FRANCIS *following with wine.*]

Poins Welcome, Jack: where hast thou been?

Falstaff A plague of all cowards, I say, and a ven-   115
geance too! marry, and amen! Give me a cup of
sack, boy. Ere I lead this life long, I'll sew nether
stocks and mend them and foot them too. A plague
of all cowards! Give me a cup of sack, rogue. Is
there no virtue extant? [*He drinks.*]   120

Prince Didst thou ever see Titan kiss a dish of butter? pitiful-hearted Titan, that melted at the sweet
tale of the sun's! if thou didst, then behold that
compound.

Falstaff You rogue, here's lime in this sack too: 125
there is nothing but roguery to be found in villainous
man: yet a coward is worse than a cup of sack with
lime in it. A villainous coward! Go thy ways, old
Jack; die when thou wilt, if manhood, good man-
hood, be not forgot upon the face of the earth, then   130

94.	*humours:* here means moods.
103.	*parcel of reckoning:* bill item.
112.	*Rivo:* exclamation used at drinking-bouts (perhaps of Spanish origin).
113.	*tallow:* fat.
117–8.	*nether stocks:* foot stockings.
	foot: provide feet for.
121.	*Titan:* the sun (a giant).
125.	*lime:* lime was introduced by dishonest innkeepers or their servants to restore temporary sparkle to wine that had gone flat and stale. This practice was believed to lead to stones in the bladder.

am I a shotten herring. There live not three good men
unhanged in England; and one of them is fat and
grows old: God help the while! a bad world, I say.
I would I were a weaver; I could sing psalms or any
thing. A plague of all cowards, I say still. 135

Prince How now, wool-sack! what mutter you? 136

Falstaff A king's son! If I do not beat thee out of
thy kingdom with a dagger of lath, and drive all thy
subjects afore thee like a flock of wild-geese, I'll
never wear hair on my face more. You Prince of 140
Wales!

Prince Why, you round man, what's the matter?

Falstaff Are not you a coward? answer me to that:
and Poins there?

Poins 'Zounds, ye fat paunch, an ye call me cow- 145
ard, by the Lord, I'll stab thee.

Falstaff I call thee coward! I'll see thee damned
ere I call thee coward: but I would give a thousand
pound I could run as fast as thou canst. You are
straight enough in the shoulders, you care not who 150
sees your back: call you that backing of your
friends? A plague upon such backing! give me them
that will face me. Give me a cup of sack: I am a
rogue, if I drunk to-day.

Prince O villain! thy lips are scarce wiped since 155
thou drunkest last.

Falstaff All's one for that. [*He drinks.*] A plague
of all cowards, still say I.

Prince What's the matter?

Falstaff What's the matter! there be four of us 160
here have ta'en a thousand pound this day morning.

Prince Where is it, Jack? where is it?

Falstaff Where is it! taken from us it is: a hundred upon poor four of us.

Prince What, a hundred, man? 165

Falstaff I am a rogue, if I were not a half-sword

131. *shotten herring:* female herring after it has released
all of its eggs and therefore appears lean.

136. *wool-sack:* large woolen cushion.

138. *lath:* strip of wood.

145. *'Zounds:* by God's (Christ's) wounds.

166. *a half-sword:* close fighting.

with a dozen of them two hours together. I have
'scaped by miracle. I am eight times thrust through
the doublet, four through the hose; my buckler cut
through and through; my sword hacked like a hand-   170
saw — *ecce signum*! I never dealt better since I was
a man: all would not do. A plague of all cowards!
Let them speak: if they speak more or less than
truth; they are villains and the sons of darkness.

Prince Speak, sirs: how was it?   175

Gadshill We four set upon some dozen —

Falstaff Sixteen at least, my lord.

Gadshill And bound them.

Peto No, no, they were not bound.

Falstaff You rogue, they were bound, every man of   180
them; or I am a Jew else, an Ebrew Jew.

Gadshill As we were sharing, some six or seven
fresh men set upon us —

Falstaff And unbound the rest, and then come in
the other.   185

Prince What, fought you with them all?

Falstaff All! I know not what you call all? but if I
fought not with fifty of them, I am a bunch of rad-
ish: if there were not two or three and fifty upon
poor old Jack, then am I no two-legged creature.   190

Prince Pray God you have not murdered some of
them.

Falstaff Nay, that's past praying for: I have peppered two of them; two I am sure I have paid, two
rogues in buckram suits. I tell thee what, Hal, if I   195
tell thee a lie, spit in my face, call me horse. Thou
knowest my old ward; here I lay, and thus I bore
my point. Four rogues in buckram let drive at me —

Prince What, four? thou saidst but two even now.

Falstaff Four, Hal; I told thee four.   200

Poins Ay, ay, he said four.

Falstaff These four came all a-front, and mainly

---

169. *doublet:* lined jacket.

hose: either long stockings or close fitting knee-breeches.

buckler: shield.

171. *ecce signum:* Latin for "behold the evidence."

181. *Ebrew:* Hebrew.

193. *peppered:* sprinkled with holes like a pepper shaker top.

195. *buckram:* coarse linen stiffened with gum or paste.

thrust at me. I made me no more ado but took all
their seven points in my target, thus.

Prince Seven? why, there were but four even now.   205

Falstaff In buckram?

Poins Ay, four, in buckram suits.

Falstaff Seven, by these hilts, or I am a villain else.

Prince Prithee, let him alone; we shall have more
anon.   210

Falstaff Dost thou hear me. Hal?

Prince Ay, and mark thee too, Jack.

Falstaff Do so, for it is worth the listening to.
These nine in buckram that I told thee of —

Prince So, two more already.   215

Falstaff Their points being broken, —

Poins Down fell their hose.

Falstaff Began to give me ground: but I followed
me close, came in foot and hand; and with a thought
seven of the eleven I paid.   220

Prince O monstrous! eleven buckram men grown
out of two!

Falstaff But, as the devil would have it, three mis-
begotten knaves in Kendal green came at my back
and let drive at me; for it was so dark, Hal, that thou   225
couldst not see thy hand.

Prince These lies are like their father that begets
them; gross as a mountain, open, palpable. Why,
thou not-pated fool, thou obscene, greasy tallow-
keech —   230

Falstaff What, art thou mad? art thou mad? is not
the truth the truth?

Prince Why, how couldst thou know these men in
Kendal green, when it was so dark thou couldst not
see thy hand? come, tell us your reason: what sayest   235
thou to this?

Poins Come, your reason, Jack, your reason.

204. *target:* shield.

212. *mark:* (1) notice; (2) count.

216. *points:* here used in a double sense to mean (1) tips
of swords and (2) braces, or suspenders used to
keep up breeches.

224. *Kendal green:* olive green wool cloth manufactured
at Kendal, a town in the old English county of
Westmorland.

228. *palpable:* capable of being touched.

230. *keech:* the fat of a slaughtered animal.

Falstaff What, upon compulsion? 'Zounds, an I
were at the strappado, or all the racks in the world,
I would not tell you on compulsion. Give you a rea-   240
son on compulsion! if reasons were as plentiful as
blackberries, I would give no man a reason upon
compulsion, I.

Prince I'll be no longer guilty of this sin; this san-
guine coward, this horseback-breaker, this huge hill   245
of flesh, —

Falstaff 'Sblood, you starveling, you eel-skin, you
dried neat's tongue, you stock-fish! O for breath to
utter what is like thee! you tailor's yard, you sheath,
you bow-case, you vile standing-tuck, —   250

Prince Well, breathe awhile, and then to it again:
and when thou hast tired thyself in base compari-
sons, hear me speak but this.

Poins Mark, Jack.

Prince We two saw you four set on four and bound   255
them, and were masters of their wealth. Mark now,
how a plain tale shall put you down. Then did we
two set on you four; and, with a word, out-faced you
from your prize, and have it; yea, and can show it
you here in the house: and, Falstaff, you carried   260
yourself away as nimbly, with as quick dexterity,
and roared for mercy and still run and roared, as
ever I heard bull-calf. What a slave art thou, to hack
thy sword as thou hast done, and then say it was in
fight! What trick, what device, what starting-hole,   265
canst thou now find out to hide thee from this open
and apparent shame?

Poins Come, let's hear Jack; what trick hast thou
now?

Falstaff By the Lord, I knew ye as well as he that   270
made ye. Why, hear you, my masters: was it for me
to kill the heir-apparent? should I turn upon the
true prince? why, thou knowest I am as valiant as
Hercules: but beware instinct; the lion will not
touch the true Prince. Instinct is a great matter; I   275
was now a coward on instinct. I shall think the better

239. *strappado:* torture in which the victim has his hands tied to a rope behind his back and is lifted up and dropped so his body weight dislocates his shoulders.

248. *neat's tongue:* ox-tongue.

stock-fish: dried cod.

249. *yard:* measuring rod.

250. *standing-tuck:* blade that has lost its tempering.

265. *starting-hole:* bolt-hole.

274. *Hercules:* mythological strongman.

of myself and thee during my life; I for a valiant
lion, and thou for a true Prince. But, by the Lord,
lads, I am glad you have the money. Hostess, clap
to the doors: watch to-night, pray to-morrow. Gal-   280
lants, lads, boys, hearts of gold, all the titles of good
fellowship come to you! What, shall we be merry?
shall we have a play extempore?

Prince Content; and the argument shall be thy running away.   285

Falstaff Ah, no more of that, Hal, an thou lovest
me.

[*Enter* Hostess.]

Hostess O Jesu, my lord the prince!

Prince How now, my lady the hostess! what sayest
thou to me?   290

Hostess Marry, my lord, there is a nobleman of the
court at door would speak with you: he says he
comes from your father.

Prince Give him as much as will make him a royal
man, and send him back again to my mother.   295

Falstaff What manner of man is he?

Hostess An old man.

Falstaff What doth gravity out of his bed at midnight? Shall I give him his answer?

Prince Prithee, do, Jack.   300

Falstaff 'Faith, and I'll send him packing. [*Exit*]

Prince Now, sirs: by'r lady, you fought fair; so did
you, Peto; so did you, Bardolph: you are lions too,
you ran away upon instinct, you will not touch the
true prince; no, fie!   305

Bardolph 'Faith, I ran when I saw others run.

Prince 'Faith, tell me now in earnest, how came
Falstaff's sword so hacked?

Peto Why, he hacked it with his dagger, and said
he would swear truth out of England but he would   310

280. *watch:* (1) keep on guard; (2) stay up late (drinking).

283. *extempore:* unrehearsed (on the spur of the moment).

284. *argument:* plot.

make you believe it was done in fight, and persuaded us to do the like.

Bardolph Yea, and to tickle our noses with spear-grass to make them bleed, and then to beslubber our garments with it and swear it was the blood of true men. I did that I did not this seven year before, I blushed to hear his monstrous devices.

Prince O villain, thou stolest a cup of sack eighteen years ago, and wert taken with the manner, and ever since thou hast blushed extempore. Thou hadst fire and sword on thy side, and yet thou rannest away: what instinct hadst thou for it?

Bardolph My lord, do you see these meteors? Do you behold these exhalations?

Prince I do.

Bardolph What think you they portend?

Prince Hot livers and cold purses.

Bardolph Choler, my lord, if rightly taken.

Prince No, if rightly taken, halter.

[*Re-enter* FALSTAFF.]
Here comes lean Jack, here comes bare-bone. How now, my sweet creature of bombast! How long is't ago, Jack, since thou sawest thine own knee?

Falstaff My own knee? when I was about thy years, Hal, I was not an eagle's talon in the waist; I could have crept into any alderman's thumb-ring: a plague of sighing and grief! it blows a man up like a bladder. There's villainous news abroad: here was Sir John Bracy from your father; you must to the court in the morning. That same mad fellow of the north, Percy, and he of Wales, that gave Amamon the bastinado and swore the devil his true ligeman upon the cross of a Welsh hook — what a plague call you him?

Poins O, Glendower.

Falstaff Owen, Owen, the same; and his son-in-law Mortimer, and old Northumberland, and that

315

320

325

330

335

340

345

313.	*spear-grass:* coarse grass.
322.	*instinct:* a reference to Falstaff's previous use of this word as his excuse for not hurting the true prince.
324.	*exhalations:* shooting stars. (Bardolph likens the boils on his face to them. Meteors were thought to be bad omens.)
329.	*rightly taken:* properly understood.
328–9.	*Choler . . . halter:* pun on collar and the hangman's noose. The whole play is full of references, mostly oaths or puns, to the act of hanging.
330.	*lean Jack:* another ironic reference to Falstaff's corpulence.
340.	*Amamon:* name of a fiend (perhaps a corruption of the Greek name Agamemnon).
340.	*bastinado:* thrashing or cudgeling.
342.	*Welsh hook:* a weapon made from a pruning hook attached to a long staff.

sprightly Scot of Scots, Douglas, that runs o' horseback up a hill perpendicular, —

Prince He that rides at high speed and with his
pistol kills a sparrow flying.

Falstaff You have hit it.   350

Prince So did he never the sparrow.

Falstaff Well, that rascal hath good mettle in him;
he will not run.

Prince Why, what a rascal art thou then, to praise
him so for running!   355

Falstaff O' horseback, ye cuckoo; but afoot he will
not budge a foot.

Prince Yes, Jack, upon instinct.

Falstaff I grant ye, upon instinct. Well, he is there
too, and one Mordake, and a thousand blue-caps   360
more: Worcester is stolen away to-night; thy father's
beard is turned white with the news: you may buy
land now as cheap as stinking mackerel. But tell
me, Hal, art not thou horrible afeard? thou being
heir-apparent, could the world pick thee out three   365
such enemies again as that fiend Douglas, that spirit
Percy, and the devil Glendower? Art thou not horribly afraid? doth not thy blood thrill at it?

Prince Not a whit, i' faith; lack some of thy in-
stinct.   370

Falstaff Well, thou wilt be horribly chid to-morrow
when thou comest to thy father: if thou love me,
practise an answer.

Prince Do thou stand for my father, and examine
me upon the particulars of my life.   375

Falstaff Shall I? content: this chair shall be my
state, this dagger my sceptre, and this cushion my
crown.

Prince Thy state is taken for a joint-stool, thy gold-
en sceptre for a leaden dagger, and thy precious   380
rich crown for a pitiful bald crown.

349. *pistol:* an anachronism, because pistols were not in use during Henry IV's reign.

362–3. *you may buy land now as cheap as stinking mackerel:* land prices have fallen because of civil instability.

371. *chid:* told off.

Falstaff Well, an the fire of grace be not quite out
of thee, now shalt thou be moved. Give me a cup of
sack to make my eyes look red, that it may be
thought I have wept; for I must speak in passion, 385
and I will do it in King Cambyses' vein.

Prince Well, here is my leg.

Falstaff And here is my speech. Stand aside, nobility.

Hostess O Jesu, this is excellent sport, i' faith! 390

Falstaff Weep not, sweet queen; for trickling tears
are vain.

Hostess O, the father, how he holds his countenance!

Falstaff For God's sake, lords, convey my tristful 395
queen; For tears do stop the flood-gates of her eyes.

Hostess O Jesu, he doth it as like one of these
players as ever I see!

Falstaff Peace, good pint-pot; peace, good tickle-
brain. Harry, I do not only marvel where thou 400
spendest thy time but also how thou art accompanied: for though the camomile, the more it is trodden on the faster it grows, yet youth, the more it is
wasted the sooner it wears. That thou art my son, I
have partly thy mother's word, partly my own opin- 405
ion, but chiefly a villainous trick of thine eye and a
foolish hanging of thy nether lip, that doth warrant
me. If then thou be son to me, here lies the point;
why, being son to me, art thou so pointed at? Shall
the blessed sun of heaven prove a micher and eat 410
blackberries? a question not to be asked. Shall the
son of England prove a thief and take purses? a
question to be asked. There is a thing, Harry, which
thou hast often heard of and it is known to many in
our land by the name of pitch: this pitch, as ancient 415
writers do report, doth defile; so doth the company thou keepest: for, Harry, now I do not speak to
thee in drink but in tears, not in pleasure but in passion, not in words only, but in woes also: and yet

386. *King Cambyses' vein:* in the ranting style of a much-parodied play by Thomas Preston.

395. *tristful:* sorrowing.

410. *micher:* truant.

there is a virtuous man whom I have often noted in   420
thy company, but I know not his name.

Prince What manner of man, an it like your majesty?

Falstaff A goodly portly man, i' faith, and a corpu-
lent; of a cheerful look, a pleasing eye and a most   425
noble carriage; and, as I think, his age some fifty,
or, by'r lady inclining to three score; and now I remember me, his name is Falstaff; if that man should
be lewdly given, he deceiveth me; for, Harry, I see
virtue in his looks. If then the tree may be known by   430
the fruit, as the fruit by the tree, then, peremptorily
I speak it, there is virtue in that Falstaff: him keep
with, the rest banish. And tell me now, thou naughty
varlet, tell me, where hast thou been this month?

Prince Dost thou speak like a king? Do thou stand   435
for me, and I'll play my father.

Falstaff Depose me? If thou dost it half so gravely,
so majestically, both in word and matter, hang me
up by the heels for a rabbit-sucker or a poulter's hare.

Prince Well, here I am set.   440

Falstaff And here I stand: judge, my masters.

Prince Now, Harry, whence come you?

Falstaff My noble lord, from Eastcheap.

Prince The complaints I hear of thee are grievous.

Falstaff 'Sblood, my lord, they are false: nay, I'll   445
tickle ye for a young prince, i' faith.

Prince Swearest thou, ungracious boy? henceforth
ne'er look on me. Thou are violently carried away
from grace: there is a devil haunts thee in the likeness of an old fat man; a tun of man is thy com-   450
panion. Why dost thou converse with that trunk of
humours, that bolting-hutch of beastliness, that swol-
len parcel of dropsies, that huge bombard of sack,

437. *Depose:* he has been deposed from playing the part of the King to play the part of the Prince.

439. *rabbit-sucker:* suckling rabbit.

446. *tickle:* please.

450. *tun:* huge cask.

452. *humours:* bodily fluids. Contemporary medicine believed there to be four humors: blood, phlegm, choler, and melancholy.

bolting-hutch: receptacle for dross.

453. *dropsies:* diseased concentration of body fluids.

bombard: leather container.

that stuffed cloak-bag, that roasted Manningtree ox,
that reverend vice, that grey iniquity, that father   455
ruffian, that vanity in years? Wherein is he good,
but to taste sack and drink it? wherein neat and
cleanly, but to carve a capon and eat it? wherein cunning, but in craft? wherein crafty, but in villainy?
wherein villainous, but in all things? wherein worthy,   460
but in nothing?

Falstaff I would your grace would take me with
you: whom means your grace?

Prince That villainous abominable misleader of
youth, Falstaff, that old white-bearded Satan.   465

Falstaff My lord, the man I know.

Prince I know thou dost.

Falstaff But to say I know more harm in him than
in myself, were to say more than I know. That he is
old, the more the pity, his white hairs do witness it.   470
If sack and sugar be a fault, God help the wicked! if
to be old and merry be a sin, then many an old host
that I know is damned: if to be fat be to be hated,
then Pharaoh's lean kine are to be loved. No, my
good lord; banish Peto, banish Bardolph, banish   475
Poins: but for sweet Jack Falstaff, kind Jack Falstaff, true Jack Falstaff, valiant Jack Falstaff, and
therefore more valiant, being, as he is, old Jack Falstaff, banish not him thy Harry's company, banish
not him thy Harry's company: banish plump Jack,   480
and banish all the world.

Prince I do, I will. [*A knocking heard.*]

[*Exeunt* Hostess, FRANCIS *and* BARDOLPH.]

[*Re-enter* BARDOLPH, *running.*]

Bardolph O, my lord, my lord! the sheriff with a
most monstrous watch is at the door.

Falstaff Out, ye rogue! Play out the play: I have   485
much to say in the behalf of that Falstaff.

[*Re-enter the* Hostess.]

Hostess O Jesu my lord, my lord!

454.   *Manningtree ox:* Manning-tree in Essex was
noted for its roasted oxen at festival time.

455-456.   *vice, iniquity, vanity:* these might well have been
printed with capital letters since they are the
names of characters (personifications of various
common sins) in the old morality plays.

484.   *watch:* equivalent of police force.

Prince Heigh, heigh! the devil rides upon a fiddle-
stick: what's the matter?

Hostess The sheriff and all the watch are at the   490
door: they are come to search the house. Shall I let
them in?

Falstaff Dost thou hear, Hal? never call a true
piece of gold a counterfeit: thou are essentially mad,
without seeming so.   495

Prince And thou a natural coward, without instinct.

Falstaff I deny your major: if you will deny the
sheriff, so; if not, let him enter: if I become not a
cart as well as another man, a plague on my bringing
up! I hope I shall as soon be strangled with a halter   500
as another.

Prince Go hide thee behind the arras: the rest walk
up above. Now, my masters, for a true face and good
conscience.

Falstaff Both which I have had: but their date is   505
out, and therefore I'll hide me.

Prince Call in the sheriff.

[*Exeunt all except the* PRINCE *and* PETO.]

[*Enter* Sheriff *and the* Carrier.]
Now master sheriff, what is your will with me?

Sheriff First, pardon me, my lord. A hue and cry
Hath follow'd certain men unto this house.   510

Prince What men?

Sheriff One of them is well known, my gracious
lord,
A gross fat man.

Carrier   As fat as butter.

Prince The man, I do assure you, is not here;
For I myself at this time have employ'd him.   515
And, sheriff, I will engage my word to thee
That I will, by to-morrow dinner-time,
Send him to answer thee, or any man,
For any thing he shall be charged withal:
And so let me entreat you leave the house.   520

497.   *major:* (pronounced mayor in the Latin way at this
time) a term in logic to denote the first and most
inclusive term in the syllogism, but here used also
as a pun on sheriff, because this officer reported to
the mayor, as chief magistrate.

498–9.   *become not a cart:* if I am not a credit to the cart
(which takes me to be executed).

502.   *arras:* tapestry wall-hanging.

509.   *hue and cry:* hunting terms for shouting of alarm or
protest (from the French verb *huer*, to shout).

Sheriff I will, my lord. There are two gentlemen
Have in this robbery lost three hundred marks.

Prince It may be so: if he have robb'd these men,
He shall be answerable; and so farewell.

Sheriff Good night, my noble lord.   525

Prince I think it is good morrow, is it not?

Sheriff Indeed, my lord, I think it be two o'clock.

[*Exeunt* Sheriff *and* Carrier.]

Prince This oily rascal is known as well as Paul's.
Go, call him forth.

Peto Falstaff! — Fast asleep behind the arras, and   530
snorting like a horse.

Prince Hark, how hard he fetches breath. Search
his pockets. [*He searcheth his pockets and findeth
certain papers.*] What hast thou found?

Peto Nothing but papers, my lord.   535

Prince Let's see what they be: read them.

Peto [*Reads*] Item, A capon,   2s. 2d.
Item, Sauce,   4d.
Item, Sack, two gallons,   5s. 8d.
Item, Anchovies, and sack   540
after supper   2s. 6d.
Item, Bread,   ob.

Prince O monstrous! but one half-pennyworth of
bread to this intolerable deal of sack! What there is
else, keep close; we'll read it at more advantage: 545
there let him sleep till day. I'll to the court in the
morning. We must all to the wars, and thy place
shall be honourable. I'll procure this fat rogue a
charge of foot; and I know his death will be a march
of twelve-score. The money shall be paid back with   550
advantage. Be with me betimes in the morning; and
so good morrow, Peto. [*Exeunt.*]

Peto Good morrow, good my lord.

528.   *Paul's:* St. Paul's Cathedral, in London. Falstaff is just as dominant a landmark.

537.   *2s. 2d.:* two shillings and two pence (said, "two and tuppence").

538.   *4d.:* four pence (said, "fourpence").

539.   *5s. 8d.:* five shillings and eight pence (said, "five and eightpence").

541.   *2s. 6d.:* two shillings and six pence (said, "two and sixpence").

542.   *ob.:* "obulus," a half-penny, sometimes said as "ha'penny."

544.   *deal:* portion.

545.   *at more advantage:* at a more suitable time.

549.   *charge of foot:* commission roughly equivalent to a captaincy in the infantry.

550.   *score:* twenty. Twelve-score is thus 240.

551.   *advantage:* interest.

betimes: early.

COMMENTARY

Act II, Scene 4 is known as the first tavern scene and is the longest scene in the play. It is much praised by critics for its clever structure and for the insights it offers into several key themes. The scene falls into three parts: the comic teasing of Francis, the outcome of the joke played upon Falstaff, and the improvised role-play of Falstaff and Prince Hal.

Gamblers outside of a tavern.
Pushkin Museum of Fine Arts, Moscow/SuperStock

The Prince tells Poins how well he has been received by the tavern group at Eastcheap. He is on first-name terms with all of them and describes how they have welcomed him into their company as an equal. He might be a prince, they say, but in matters of courtesy he is a king. Hal clearly has "the common touch," and he is proud of it. He is in high spirits.

Falstaff and the others haven't yet returned, so, "to drive away the time" until they do, Prince Hal proposes another joke that he and Poins should play, this time upon Francis, one of the tavern's "drawers" (the rough equivalent of waiters or barmen). The Prince will engage Francis in a complicated conversation, which Poins will repeatedly interrupt by calling for service from an adjoining room. Poor Francis is so confused by Hal and Poins that eventually he "stands amazed, not knowing which way to go."

Hal's actions have a kind of symbolic significance. The audience knows that he is play-acting with Francis, pretending to be serious when he is not. Francis is

stupid and takes him at face value. The result is comic. But what the audience also knows is that Hal is acting a part all the time (he has said so in his soliloquy at the end of Act I, Scene 2). So Hal is acting at acting — a kind of double-take on the theme, which makes the audience think more deeply about the difference between how people appear and how people really are. And just before Falstaff and the others appear, Hal indulges in more role-play. He invents a conversation between Hotspur and his wife, parodying them both to comic effect. The audience knows how well he lampoons the Hotspurs because Shakespeare has shown them to us in the previous scene.

The second part of Act II, Scene 4, begins with the arrival of Falstaff, Gadshill, Bardolph, and Peto. Shakespeare last showed them running for their lives. Falstaff calls Poins and Prince Hal cowards for deserting them and invents a fantastic tale of how they were set upon by a huge band of robbers who relieved them of their plunder after a valiant life-and-death struggle. The audience knows all this is a lie; so do Poins and the Prince, of course. The number of assailants that Falstaff allegedly fought off grows with the telling, despite the fact that it must be obvious to everyone that he is lying. (It was so dark, he says, that you could not see your own hand; yet he claims to know the color of the clothing worn by his assailants.)

A doublet.

The Prince finally tells them the truth. The audience might expect Falstaff to be deflated by this; but, on the contrary (after, perhaps, no more than a pause for breath), he claims to have known all the while (by "instinct") that one of his attackers had been the Prince. "Why, hear you, my masters: was it for me to kill the heir-apparent?" We can only be impressed by Falstaff's brazenness. In the space of a few lines, he is off the hook and proposing that they should have some fun by acting out a play. And why not, says Prince Hal. The plot ("the argument") can be Falstaff's running away.

The Hostess tells the friends that a nobleman has arrived to give the Prince a message from his father, the King. Falstaff goes to head him off, and, when he has gone, the others admit to the tricks they used to make it look like they had been in a fierce fight. When Falstaff returns, he says that the King has summoned Hal to him and that "There's villainous news abroad": The rebels are assembling. Falstaff says that Hal is certain to be given a telling-off by his father when he goes to him, and he had better prepare himself for it; Hal suggests they act out the interview.

The scene Hal and Falstaff play out is deliciously comic, as the Hostess's delighted interjections suggest. Falstaff consciously adopts a high tragic style. His speech is full of rhetorical devices (the tricks of the trade of the formal speaker) and is beautifully structured. He brings up the subject of the low company that Hal keeps, but points out that he should stand by one of his friends, Falstaff, "A good portly man, i' faith."

They change places: Hal plays his own father, Falstaff plays Hal. Hal, acting the part of King Henry, also singles out Falstaff for comment: "there is a devil haunts thee in the likeness of an old fat man," he says, and then launches into a catalog of magnificent insults to describe him. Hal uses alliteration for emphasis ("that bolting-hutch of beastliness . . . that huge bombard of sack") and asks eight damning rhetorical questions to which he explicitly supplies the answer. Though it is obvious that this is a description of Falstaff, Falstaff (as Hal) asks (and we can imagine his quizzical pause) "whom means your grace?" Falstaff (as Hal) then speaks up for his real self, pleading that he should not be banished, but Hal (as the King) says that he will in fact do so (as, indeed, he does, when he becomes King at the end of *Henry IV, Part 2*).

A gentleman wearing hose.

This interlude is ended by the arrival of the Sheriff and his watchmen who are hunting for Falstaff and his companions. They have been followed to the tavern after the robbery. Hal assumes a princely manner and tells the Sheriff (in blank verse, appropriate to his dignity) that they are not there, although they are in fact hiding behind the arras. When the Sheriff has gone, Fastaff is found to have fallen asleep. Hal goes through his pockets and finds tavern bills. At the end of the scene, we are reminded that a war is coming: Hal says he will get his fat friend a commission in the army, which will have to be raised to fight in it. His salary will enable him to pay his huge debts.

Shakespeare develops several main themes in this long and important scene. He creates a play on the difference between appearance and reality. The Prince acts out — and enjoys — the part of a regular customer of the tavern, where he is accepted on equal terms. He acts out a joke upon poor Francis, the apprentice drawer. He imitates the speech and mannerisms of Hotspur and his wife, and he jokingly plays out the part of his father. These variations on the idea of pretending to be what one is not are too many to be coincidental.

The relationship of fathers and sons is also taken further. Once more, comedy and seriousness combine, for as we laugh at the way that Hal and Falstaff tease each other in their play-acting of the coming encounter between Hal and his father, the King, we are also aware that the Prince has determined to "reform" and abandon his irresponsible life. That life, of course, includes Falstaff; the audience naturally begins to feel unsettled at the prospect of this delightful friendship coming to an end. Meanwhile, Hal continues to show loyalty to Falstaff in hiding him from the Sheriff.

The original St Paul's Cathedral dominated the skyline of medieval London. It was burned down in the great fire of 1666, and its replacement designed by Sir Christopher Wren.
SuperStock

Notes

King *And in that very line, Harry, standest thou;*
For thou hast lost thy princely privilege
With vile participation: not an eye
But is a-weary of thy common sight,
Save mine, which hath desired to see thee more;
Which now doth that I would not have it do,
Make blind itself with foolish tenderness.

Prince *I shall hereafter, my thrice gracious lord,*
Be more myself.

Act III, Scene 1

The rebels meet, and Glendower and Hotspur argue. They decide how they will divide up the kingdom when they have defeated the King. The wives of Glendower and Hotspur show their contrasting characters.

ACT III, SCENE 1
Bangor, the Archdeacon's house.

[*Enter* HOTSPUR, WORCESTER, MORTIMER, *and* GLENDOWER.]

Mortimer These promises are fair, the parties sure,
And our induction full of prosperous hope.

Hotspur Lord Mortimer, and cousin Glendower,
Will you sit down?
And uncle Worcester: a plague upon it!　　　　　　　　　5
I have forgot the map.

Glendower　　　　　　No, here it is.
Sit, cousin Percy; sit, good cousin Hotspur,
For by that name as oft as Lancaster
Doth speak of you, his check looks pale and with
A rising sigh he wisheth you in heaven.　　　　　　　10

Hotspur And you in hell as often as he hears
Owen Glendower spoke of.

Glendower I cannot blame him: at my nativity
The front of heaven was full of fiery shapes,
Of burning cressets: and at my birth　　　　　　　　15
The frame and huge foundation of the earth
Shaked like a coward.

Hotspur Why, so it would have done at the same
season, if your mother's cat had but kittened, though
yourself had never been born.　　　　　　　　　　　20

Glendower I say the earth did shake when I was
born.

Hotspur And I say the earth was not of my mind,
If you suppose as fearing you it shook.

NOTES

1.　*promises:* i.e., those made by rebel-sympathizers in different parts of the country to send support.

2.　*induction:* being lead in to claim the throne at the coronation.

8.　*Lancaster:* Henry IV's family name from the dukedom of Lancaster.

14.　*front:* forehead.

15.　*cressets:* open lamp or fire-basket set up to a beacon (used figuratively here).

Glendower The heavens were all on fire, the earth   25
    did tremble.

Hotspur O, then the earth shook to see the heavens
       on fire,
    And not in fear of your nativity.
    Diseased nature oftentimes breaks forth
    In strange eruptions; oft the teeming earth
    Is with a kind of colic pinch'd and vex'd   30
    By the imprisoning of unruly wind
    Within her womb; which, for enlargement striving,
    Shakes the old beldam earth and topples down
    Steeples and moss-grown towers. At your birth
    Our grandam earth, having this distemperature,   35
    In passion shook.

Glendower   Cousin, of many men
    I do not bear these crossings. Give me leave
    To tell you once again that at my birth
    The front of heaven was full of fiery shapes,
    The goats ran from the mountains, and the herds   40
    Were strangely clamorous to the frighted fields.
    These signs have mark'd me extraordinary
    And all the courses of my life do show
    I am not in the roll of common men.
    Where is he living, clipp'd in with the sea   45
    That chides the banks of England, Scotland, Wales,
    Which calls me pupil, or hath read to me?
    And bring him out that is but woman's son
    Can trace me in the tedious ways of art
    And hold me pace in deep experiments.   50

Hotspur I think there's no man speaks better
       Welsh.
    I'll to dinner.

Mortimer Peace, cousin Percy; you will make him
       mad.

Glendower I can call spirits from the vasty deep.

Hotspur Why, so can I, or so can any man;   55
    But will they come when you do call for them?

---

33. *beldam:* grandmother (note the sustained metaphor to describe earthquakes).

35. *distemperature:* illness or other physical disorder.

37. *crossings:* contradictions.

41. *clamorous:* crying aloud.

frighted fields: transferred epithet.

44. *roll:* book of names (used figuratively).

45. *clipp'd in:* surrounded by.

46. *chides:* the angry vehemence and lashing of water.

50. *hold me pace in deep experiments:* keep up with me in deep magic.

Glendower Why, I can teach you, cousin, to com-
    mand
  The devil.

Hotspur And I can teach thee, coz to shame the
    devil
  By telling truth: to tell truth and shame the devil.   60
  If thou have power to raise him, bring him hither,
  And I'll be sworn I have power to shame him hence.
  O, while you live, tell truth and shame the devil!

Mortimer Come, come, no more of this unprofitable
    chat.

Glendower Three times hath Henry Bolingbroke   65
    made head
  Against my power; thrice from the banks of Wye
  And sandy-bottom'd Severn have I sent him
  Bootless home and weather-beaten back.

Hotspur Home without boots, and in foul weather
    too!
  How 'scapes he agues, in the devil's name?   70

Glendower Come, here's the map: shall we divide
    our right
  According to our threefold order ta'en?

Mortimer The archdeacon hath divided it
  Into three limits very equally:
  England, from Trent and Severn hitherto,   75
  By south and east is to my part assign'd:
  All westward, Wales beyond the Severn shore,
  And all the fertile land within that bound,
  To Owen Glendower: and, dear coz, to you
  The remnant northward, lying off from Trent.   80
  And our indentures tripartite are drawn;
  Which being sealed interchangeably,
  A business that this night may execute,
  To-morrow, cousin Percy, you and I
  And my good Lord of Worcester will set forth   85
  To meet your father and the Scottish power,
  As is appointed us, at Shrewsbury.

65. *made head:* brought together an armed force for the purpose of attacking.

66. *power:* army.

70. *agues:* fevers.

81. *indentures tripartite:* contract drawn up in triplicate (by the Archdeacon).

My father Glendower is not ready yet,
Nor shall we need his help these fourteen days.
Within that space you may have drawn together 90
Your tenants, friends and neighbouring gentlemen.

Glendower A shorter time shall send me to you,
      lords:
And in my conduct shall your ladies come:
From whom you now must steal and take no leave,
For there will be a world of water shed 95
Upon the parting of your wives and you.

Hotspur Methinks my moiety, north from Burton
      here,
In quantity equals not one of yours:
See how this river comes me cranking in,
And cuts me from the best of all my land 100
A huge half-moon, a monstrous cantle out.
I'll have the current in this place damm'd up;
And here the smug and silver Trent shall run
In a new channel, fair and evenly;
It shall not wind with such a deep indent, 105
To rob me of so rich a bottom here.

Glendower Not wind? it shall, it must, you see it
      doth.

Mortimer Yea, but
Mark how he bears his course, and runs me up
With like advantage on the other side; 110
Gelding the opposed continent as much
As on the other side it takes from you.

Worcester Yea, but a little charge will trench him
      here
And on this north side win this cape of land;
And then he runs straight and even. 115

Hotspur I'll have it so: a little charge will do it.

Glendower I'll not have it alter'd.

Hotspur   Will not you?

Glendower No, nor you shall not.

88. *father:* short for father-in-law.

97. *moiety:* share or portion (not half, since more than two parts are involved).

99. *cranking:* winding.

101. *cantle:* literally, corner-piece or segment of a sphere.

111. *Gelding:* depriving of an essential part.

Hotspur   Who shall say me nay?

Glendower Why, that will I.

Hotspur Let me not understand you, then; speak it   120
   in Welsh.

Glendower I can speak English, lord, as well as you;
   For I was train'd up in the English court;
   Where, being but young, I framed to the harp
   Many an English ditty lovely well
   And gave the tongue a helpful ornament,   125
   A virtue that was never seen in you.

Hotspur Marry,
   And I am glad of it with all my heart:
   I had rather be a kitten and cry mew
   Than one of these same metre ballad-mongers;   130
   I had rather hear a brazen canstick turn'd,
   Or a dry wheel grate on the axle-tree;
   And that would set my teeth nothing on edge,
   Nothing so much as mincing poetry:
   'Tis like the forced gait of a shuffling nag.   135

Glendower Come, you shall have Trent turn'd.

Hotspur I do not care: I'll give thrice so much land
   To any well-deserving friend;
   But in the way of bargain, mark ye me,
   I'll cavil on the ninth part of a hair.   140
   Are the indentures drawn? shall we be gone?

Glendower The moon shines fair; you may away
     by night:
   I'll haste the writer and withal
   Break with your wives of your departure hence:
   I am afraid my daughter will run mad,   145
   So much she doteth on her Mortimer. [*Exit.*]

Mortimer Fie, cousin Percy! how you cross my
     father!

Hotspur I cannot choose: sometime he angers me
   With telling me of the moldwarp and the ant,
   Of the dreamer Merlin and his prophecies,   150

---

124. *lovely well:* a Welsh idiom.

126. *virtue:* skill or art here.

130. *ballad-mongers:* contemptuous term for ballad-makers.

131. *canstick:* short form for candlestick (turned on a lathe, a noisy process).

132. *grate:* scrape loudly.

134. *mincing:* affected.

140. *cavil:* raise trivial objections.

149. *moldwarp:* mole (the animal).

150. *Merlin:* magician who aided King Arthur.

And of a dragon and a finless fish,
A clip-wing'd griffin and a moulten raven,
A couching lion and a ramping cat,
And such a deal of skimble-skamble stuff
As puts me from my faith. I tell you what;   155
He held me last night at least nine hours
In reckoning up the several devils' names
That were his lackeys; I cried 'hum,' and 'well, go to,'
But mark'd him not a word. O, he is as tedious
As a tired horse, a railing wife;   160
Worse than a smoky house: I had rather live
With cheese and garlic in a windmill, far,
Than feed on cates and have him talk to me
In any summer-house in Christendom.

Mortimer In faith, he is a worthy gentleman,   165
Exceedingly well read, and profited
In strange concealments, valiant as a lion
And wondrous affable and as bountiful
As mines of India. Shall I tell you, cousin?
He holds your temper in high respect   170
And curbs himself even of his natural scope
When you come 'cross his humour; faith, he does:
I warrant you, that man is not alive
Might so have tempted him as you have done,
Without the taste of danger and reproof: 175
But do not use it oft, let me entreat you.

Worcester In faith, my lord, you are too wilful-
        blame;
And since your coming hither have done enough
To put him quite beside his patience.
You must needs learn, lord, to amend this fault: 180
Though sometimes it show greatness, courage,
        blood —
And that's the dearest grace it renders you —
Yet oftentimes it doth present harsh rage,
Defect of manners, want of government,
Pride, haughtiness, opinion and disdain: 185
The least of which haunting a nobleman

152. *griffin:* mythical creature with the head, wings, and forelegs of an eagle, and the body, hind legs, and tail of a lion.

moulten: having moulted.

153. *couching:* lying down.

ramping: rearing up (from heraldic terms "rampant" and "couchant").

154. *skimble-skamble stuff:* confused, rambling nonsense.

160. *railing:* nagging.

163. *cates:* dainties, delicacies.

177. *wilful-blame:* deliberately provoking, and to be blamed for being so.

Loseth men's hearts and leaves behind a stain
Upon the beauty of all parts besides,
Beguiling them of commendation.

Hotspur Well, I am school'd: good manners be   190
    your speed!
Here come our wives, and let us take our leave.

[*Re-enter* GLENDOWER *with the* Ladies.]

Mortimer This is the deadly spite that angers me.
  My wife can speak no English, I no Welsh.

Glendower My daughter weeps: she will not part
    with you;
She'll be a soldier too, she'll to the wars.   195

Mortimer Good father, tell her that she and my
    Aunt Percy
Shall follow in your conduct speedily.

[GLENDOWER *speaks to her in Welsh, and she answers him in
  the same.*]

Glendower She is desperate here; a peevish self-
    willed thing,
That no persuasion can do good upon.

[*The lady speaks in Welsh.*]

Mortimer I understand thy looks: that pretty Welsh   200
  Which thou pour'st down from these swelling heavens
  I am too perfect in; and, but for shame,
  In such a parley should I answer thee.

[*The lady speaks again in Welsh.*]
  I understand thy kisses and thou mine,
  And that's a feeling disputation: 205
  But I will never be a truant, love,
  Till I have learn'd thy language; for thy tongue
  Makes Welsh as sweet as ditties highly penn'd,
  Sung by a fair queen in a summer's bower,
  With ravishing division, to her lute.   210

Glendower Nay, if you melt, then will she run mad.

---

190. *school'd:* disciplined as by a schoolmaster.

196. *Aunt Percy:* Kate (Hotspur's wife).

198. *peevish:* cross, fretful, complaining.

203. *parley:* conversation.

208. *ditties highly penn'd:* lyrics written in a courtly cavalier style or by courtiers of high birth, or both.

210. *division:* complex (melodic) variation.

    lute: stringed instrument like a small guitar.

[The lady speaks again in Welsh.]

Mortimer O, I am ignorance itself in this!

Glendower She bids you on the rushes lay you
    down
And rest your gentle head upon her lap,
And she will sing the song that pleaseth you   215
And on your eyelids crown the god of sleep,
Charming your blood with pleasing heaviness,
Making such difference 'twixt wake and sleep
As is the difference betwixt day and night
The hour before the heavenly-harness'd team   220
Begins his golden progress in the east.

Mortimer With all my heart I'll sit and hear her
    sing:
By that time will our book, I think, be drawn.

Glendower Do so;
And those musicians that shall play to you   225
Hang in the air a thousand leagues from hence,
And straight they shall be here: sit, and attend.

Hotspur Come, Kate, thou art perfect in lying
down: come, quick, quick, that I may lay my head in
thy lap.   230

Lady Percy Go, ye giddy goose. *[The music plays.]*

Hotspur Now I perceive the devil understands
    Welsh;
And 'tis no marvel he is so humorous.
By'r lady, he is a good musician.

Lady Percy Then should you be nothing but musi-   235
cal, for you are altogether governed by humours. Lie
still, ye thief, and hear the lady sing in Welsh.

Hotspur I had rather hear Lady, my brach, howl in
Irish.

Lady Percy Wouldst thou have thy head broken?

Hotspur No.   240

233.   *humorous:* moody.

236.   *humours:* moods.

238.   *brach:* female hunting dog.

Lady Percy Then be still.

Hotspur Neither; 'tis a woman's fault.

Lady Percy Now God help thee! What's that?

Hotspur Peace! she sings.

[*Here the lady sings a Welsh song.*]

Hotspur Come, Kate, I'll have your song too.　　　　　　245

Lady Percy Not mine, in good sooth.

Hotspur Not yours, in good sooth! Heart! you
　　swear like a comfit-maker's wife. 'Not you, in good
　　sooth', and 'as true as I live', and 'as God shall mend
　　me', and 'as sure as day'.　　　　　　　　　　250
　　And givest such sarcenet surety for thy oaths,
　　As if thou never walk'st further than Finsbury.
　　Swear me, Kate, like a lady as thou art.
　　A good mouth-filling oath, and leave 'in sooth',
　　And such protest of pepper-gingerbread,　　　255
　　To velvet-guards and Sunday-citizens.
　　Come, sing.

Lady Percy I will not sing.

Hotspur 'Tis the next way to turn tailor, or be red-
　　breast teacher. An the indentures be drawn, I'll away　　260
　　within these two hours; and so, come in when ye will.

[*Exit.*]

Glendower Come, come, Lord Mortimer; you are
　　　　as slow
　　As hot Lord Percy is on fire to go.
　　By this our book is drawn; we'll but seal,
　　And then to horse immediately.　　　　　　265

Mortimer　　　　　　　　　　With all my heart. [*Exeunt.*]

248. *comfit-maker's:* sweetmeat or confectionery-maker's.

251. *sarcenet:* fine, soft silk material.

252. *Finsbury:* Finsbury Fields, a popular place of recreation for Londoners.

254. *'in sooth':* "in truth," a very mild oath.

255. *protest of pepper-gingerbread:* exclamations that make only a little hotness in the mouth.

256. *velvet-guards:* wearers of velvet trimmings or such finery.

259–260. *red-breast:* robin. The idea is that robins are naturally well-dressed, unlike people.

264. *but:* only, just.

　　seal: affix wax seals in confirmation of the signed agreement.

COMMENTARY

In Act III, Scene 1, the play returns to the main plot. The rebels are meeting, and Mortimer's first speech sums up their optimism. Hotspur begins to speak courteously to the others but immediately interrupts himself with a flash of impetuous bad temper: "a plague upon it! I have forgot the map." Note that he is just as quick to jump to conclusions in little things as in big ones. He hasn't forgotten the map at all; it was there all the time. If he'd looked before speaking, he'd have found it.

Shakespeare brings in Owen Glendower for the first time in this scene. In Act 1, Scene 1, Westmoreland says that Glendower is "irregular and wild." Now the audience can judge for themselves. Glendower is certainly full of himself, and it is soon clear that he and Hotspur aren't going to get along well together, because each, in his way, is an egotist.

Glendower also begins with courtesy, complimenting Hotspur at the fear King Henry shows when his name is mentioned. Hotspur returns the compliment, saying that Henry is equally wary of Glendower; Glendower replies that he can't blame the King for being wary of him, because his birth was marked by fantastic omens. Hotspur scoffs at this, and they argue. Glendower says that he wouldn't put up with this sort of contradiction from most people, for he is "not in the roll of common men." With sweeping arrogance, he asks, "Where is he living . . . Which calls me pupil, or hath read to me?"

Merlin, the legendary wizard who aided King Arthur.
Newberry Library, Chicago/SuperStock

Hotspur can't stand Glendower's self-importance, and is rudely dismissive of his claims. A wiser man would perhaps have tolerated such egotism, or even flattered it; after all, the rebels need Glendower's support. But Hotspur is, as ever, impetuous and intolerant. When Glendower reminds them that he has three times repulsed the King's attacks, Hotspur turns his words into a joke.

The rebel leaders then look at the map of the kingdom, which the archdeacon has divided into three, so that when the King is defeated, each of them can rule a part of it. Hotspur instantly complains that his share is less than the others', because the River Trent, which has been chosen as one of his boundaries, makes a large loop that robs him of an area of land. Mortimer points out that the river also loops the other way at another point, making up for that loss. Worcester says that the course of the river could be straightened, and Glendower objects at first, but then gives in, only for Hotspur to say he does not care about it after all; he only wanted to win the argument. Glendower leaves to tell their womenfolk that they will soon be departing.

All this bodes ill for the rebel cause. The clash of personalities between Hotspur and Glendower is ominous. Hotspur shows neither tact nor good sense. Glendower is more flexible, but he is also proud, and Hotspur insults his pride directly, speaking contemptuously of his language and his artistic achievements. While Glendower is away, Hotspur explains to Mortimer and Worcester why he can't stand Glendower. Hotspur can't tolerate Glendower's talk of signs and portents "And such a deal of skimble-skamble stuff."

Mortimer tries to persuade him to consider Glendower's virtues: He is scholarly, has mystical insights, and is brave and generous. Moreover, he has shown Hotspur great respect by putting up with his insults. He shouldn't push his luck. Worcester agrees: "In faith, my lord, you are too wilful-blame," that is, too quick to criticize. Willfulness can sometimes be a good quality in a leader, but it can also show pettiness, too. Hotspur's response — "Well, I am school'd" — is almost certainly ironic.

An Elizabethan lute.
Musee de Louvre, Paris/Giraudon, Paris/SuperStock

Glendower returns with the ladies, and Mortimer expresses sorrow that his wife can speak no English, and that he cannot understand her Welsh. Glendower translates for his daughter and son-in-law. She wants to sing to comfort him. They are obviously very much in love, despite the language problem, and treat each other with affection and gentleness.

Hotspur and Kate have a rather different kind of relationship. Hotspur bluntly complains to her that he can't stand the sound of the Welsh singing and the music and asks her to sing something for him. He complains that she curses too gently; he would rather that she swore "A good mouth-filling oath." She refuses to sing; they all leave.

This scene is an important one, because it shows the essential disunity of the rebels. Hotspur and Glendower are clearly never going to get along. Shakespeare illustrates this not just by the way that they argue, but by the very different ways in which they relate to their wives.

Language, too, sets them apart. Hotspur can't speak Welsh, and despises it; Glendower can speak English, though, and very poetically. Hotspur despises that, too: He does not respect fine or gentle sentiments. Their diction (the kind of vocabulary they use) is very different. Glendower's speeches are full of grandiose words and phrases. He repeatedly refers to himself in the context of "heaven." Although its primary meaning here is "the skies," it also suggests that he thinks of himself as recognized by Heaven itself as having a grand and fateful role to play. Hotspur's language is far more blunt and down-to-earth, and that's how he likes it to be — hence his remarks about swearing to Kate.

Shakespeare expresses the clash of characters through this clash of languages. A neat example of this comes in lines 57–59, when Glendower addresses Hotspur as "you, cousin" and is replied to as "thee, coz." Respectful formality is answered by over-familiarity amounting to rudeness. Glendower is, after all, Hotspur's elder.

There is a deeper significance to all this disunity. One of Shakespeare's main themes in this play — and, indeed, in many others — is the problem of kingship (see the "Introduction" for more on this crucial topic). We are left in no doubt after this scene that if the rebels succeed in their plan to overthrow the King, chaos will follow.

Act III, Scene 2

The King confronts Hal with his faults. The Prince promises to mend his ways, and the King agrees to give him a command in the army that will be raised to fight the rebels.

ACT III, SCENE 2
London, the palace.

[Enter the KING, PRINCE OF WALES, *and* Others.]

King Lords, give us leave: the Prince of Wales
    and I
Must have some private conference; but be near at
    hand,
For we shall presently have need of you.

[Exeunt Lords.]
I know not whether God will have it so,
For some displeasing service I have done,   5
That, in his secret doom, out of my blood
He'll breed revengement and a scourge for me;
But thou dost in thy passages of life
Make me believe that thou art only mark'd
For the hot vengeance and the rod of heaven   10
To punish my mistreadings. Tell me else,
Could such inordinate and low desires,
Such poor, such bare, such lewd, such mean attempts,
Stuch barren pleasures, rude society,
As thou art match'd withal and grafted to,   15
Accompany the greatness of thy blood
And hold their level with thy princely heart?

Prince So please your majesty, I would I could
    Quit all offences with as clear excuse
As well as I am doubtless I can purge   20
Myself of many I am charged withal:
Yet such extenuation let me beg,
As, in reproof of many tales devised,
Which oft the ear of greatness needs must hear,
By smiling pick-thanks and base newsmongers,   25

NOTES

1.   *give us leave:* kindly leave us.

6.   *doom:* judgment.

8.   *thy passages of life:* the way you lead your life.

12.   *inordinate:* out of the limits of order.

13.   *attempts:* high jinks.

15.   *withal:* with.

     grafted: joined.

18.   *quit:* acquit myself of.

25.   *pick-thanks:* flatterers.

     newsmongers: gossips.

I may, for some things true, wherein my youth
Hath faulty wander'd and irregular,
Find pardon on my true submission.

King God pardon thee! yet let me wonder, Harry,
At thy affections, which do hold a wing   30
Quite from the flight of all thy ancestors.
Thy place in council thou hast rudely lost,
Which by thy younger brother is supplied,
And art almost an alien to the hearts
Of all the court and princes of my blood: 35
The hope and expectation of thy time
Is ruin'd, and the soul of every man
Prophetically do forethink thy fall.
Had I so lavish of my presence been,
So common-hackney'd in the eyes of men,   40
So stale and cheap to vulgar company,
Opinion, that did help me to the crown,
Had still kept loyal to possession
And left me in reputeless banishment,
A fellow of no mark nor likelihood.   45
By being seldom seen, I could not stir
But like a comet I was wonder'd at;
That men would tell their children 'This is he';
Others would say 'Where, which is Bolingbroke?'
And then I stole all courtesy from heaven,   50
And dress'd myself in such humility
That I did pluck allegiance from men's hearts,
Loud shouts and salutations from their mouths,
Even in the presence of the crowned king.
Thus did I keep my person fresh and new;   55
My presence, like a robe pontifical,
Ne'er seen but wonder'd at: and so my state,
Seldom but sumptuous, showed like a feast
And won by rareness such solemnity.
The skipping king, he ambled up and down   60
With shallow jesters and rash bavin wits,
Soon kindled and soon burnt; carded his state,
Mingled his royalty with capering fools,
Had his great name profaned with their scorns

30. *affections:* inclinations.

39. *lavish of:* free with.

40. *common-hackney'd:* ordinary, workaday.

43. *to possession:* to the possessor of it, i.e., Richard II.

44. *reputeless:* disreputable.

45. *mark:* reputation.

47. *comet:* meteor (thought to be an omen of disorder).

56. *pontifical:* pertaining to a bishop or a pope.

60. *skipping king:* gives an effect of light-heartedness and irresponsibility.

61. *bavin:* brushwood ("soon ablaze").

62. *carded:* mixed with something base.

And gave his countenance, against his name, 65
To laugh at gibing boys and stand the push
Of every beardless vain comparative,
Grew a companion to the common streets,
Enfeoff'd himself to popularity;
That, being daily swallow'd by men's eyes, 70
They surfeited with honey and began
To loathe the taste of sweetness, whereof a little
More than a little is by much too much.
So when he had occasion to be seen,
He was but as the cuckoo is in June, 75
Heard, not regarded; seen, but with such eyes
As, sick and blunted with community,
Afford no extraordinary gaze,
Such as is bent on sun-like majesty
When it shines seldom in admiring eyes; 80
But rather drowsed and hung their eyelids down,
Slept in his face and render'd such aspect
As cloudy men use to their adversaries,
Being with his presence glutted, gorged and full.
And in that very line, Harry, standest thou; 85
For thou hast lost thy princely privilege
With vile participation: not an eye
But is a-weary of thy common sight,
Save mine, which hath desired to see thee more;
Which now doth that I would not have it do, 90
Make blind itself with foolish tenderness.

Prince I shall hereafter, my thrice gracious lord,
Be more myself.

King   For all the world
As thou art to this hour was Richard then
When I from France set foot at Ravenspurgh, 95
And even as I was then is Percy now.
Now, by my sceptre and my soul to boot,
He hath more worthy interest to the state
Than thou the shadow of succession:
For of no right, nor colour like to right, 100
He doth fill fields with harness in the realm,
Turns head against the lion's armed jaws,

66. *stand the push:* put up with.

69. *Enfeoff'd himself:* surrendered himself.

75. *cuckoo:* bird common in June hence ignored.

77. *community:* commonness.

78. *Afford:* bestow.

83. *cloudy:* sullen.

87. *vile participation:* keeping company with low people.

95. *Ravenspurgh:* the port at which he landed on return from exile.

97. *to boot:* as well.

100. *colour:* appearance.

101. *harness:* armour, i.e., armed men.

And, being no more in debt to years than thou,
Leads ancient lords and reverend bishops on
To bloody battles and to bruising arms. 105
What never-dying honour hath he got
Against renowned Douglas! whose high deeds,
Whose hot incursions and great name in arms
Holds from all soldiers chief majority
And military title capital 110
Through all the kingdoms that acknowledge Christ:
Thrice hath this Hotspur, Mars in swathling clothes,
This infant warrior, in his enterprises
Discomfited great Douglas, ta'en him once,
Enlarged him and made a friend of him, 115
To fill the mouth of deep defiance up
And shake the peace and safety of our throne.
And what say you to this? Percy, Northumberland,
The Archbishop's grace of York, Douglas, Mortimer,
Capitulate against us and are up. 120
But wherefore do I tell these news to thee?
Why, Harry, do I tell thee of my foes,
Which art my near'st and dearest enemy?
Thou that art like enough, through vassal fear,
Base inclination and the start of spleen, 125
To fight against me under Percy's pay,
To dog his heels and curtsy at his frowns,
To show how much thou art degenerate.

Prince Do not think so; you shall not find it so:
And God forgive them that so much have sway'd 130
Your majesty's good thoughts away from me!
I will redeem all this on Percy's head
And in the closing of some glorious day
Be bold to tell you that I am your son;
When I will wear a garment all of blood 135
And stain my favours in a bloody mask,
Which, wash'd away, shall scour my shame with it:
And that shall be the day, whene'er it lights,
That this same child of honour and renown,
This gallant Hotspur, this all-praised knight, 140
And your unthought-of Harry chance to meet.
For every honour sitting on his helm,

109. *majority:* eminence.

112. *Mars:* god of war.
swathling clothes: wrappings of an infant.

120. *Capitulate:* draw up articles of agreement.
up: up in arms.

124. *vassal:* feudal inferior.

125. *start of spleen:* outburst of bad temper.

142. *helm:* helmet.

Would they were multitudes, and on my head
My shames redoubled! for the time will come,
That I shall make this northern youth exchange   145
His glorious deeds for my indignities.
Percy is but my factor, good my lord,
To engross up glorious deeds on my behalf;
And I will call him to so strict account,
That he shall render every glory up,   150
Yea, even the slightese worship of his time,
Or I will tear the reckoning from his heart.
This, in the name of God, I promise here:
The which if He be pleased I shall perform,
I do beseech your majesty may salve   155
The long-grown wounds of my intemperance:
If not, the end of life cancels all bands;
And I will die a hundred thousand deaths
Ere break the smallest parcel of this vow.

King A hundred thousand rebels die in this: 160
Thou shalt have charge and sovereign trust herein.

[*Enter* BLUNT.]
How now, good Blunt? thy looks are full of speed.

Blunt So hath the business that I come to speak of.
Lord Mortimer of Scotland hath sent word
That Douglas and the English rebels met   165
The eleventh of this month at Shrewsbury:
A mighty and fearful head they are,
If promises be kept on every hand,
As ever offer'd foul play in a state.

King The Earl of Westmoreland set forth to-day;   170
With him my son, Lord John of Lancaster;
For this advertisement is five days old:
On Wednesday next, Harry, you shall set forward;
On Thursday we ourselves will march: our meeting
In Bridgenorth: and, Harry, you shall march   175
Through Gloucestershire; by which account,
Our business valued, some twelve days hence
Our general forces at Bridgenorth shall meet.
Our hands are full of business: let's away:
Advantage feeds him fat while men delay. [*Exeunt.*]   180

147. *factor:* agent.
148. *engross up:* amass.
151. *worship:* honor.
155. *salve:* heal (with soothing ointment).
159. *parcel:* part.
167. *head:* military force.
172. *advertisement:* news or information.
177. *Our business valued:* when we have weighed up what we must do.

COMMENTARY

We now see the meeting between father and son for which Falstaff helped to prepare Hal in their play-acting in the last scene of Act II. The reality is far from comic. The King does not hide his disappointment in the Prince. He wonders what he has done that has led God to send him such a son as a punishment. What other explanation can there be for the undignified company Hal keeps and the dishonorable behavior that he practices? His tone is solemn, his language dignified, and they contrast strongly with the idle, merry-making manner of speech we last heard Hal and his friends using.

And yet there is dignity in Hal's reply to his father, too. Like the King, he speaks in blank verse, showing them to be on the same wavelength at last. He addresses his father respectfully, beginning. "So please your majesty," and asks to be judged on the facts, not the rumors. He is truly sorry for those faults he has shown, however, and asks forgiveness for them.

His father expresses his disappointments in him at length. Hal has been so irresponsible that his younger brother has had to take his place in the council. He is never seen at court. Everyone believes he will come to no good. If Henry had behaved like that when he was young, he would never have become king. Instead, he kept his head down and rationed his public appearances so carefully that people thought it a rare treat to catch sight of him. All this was in marked contrast to Richard II, the "skipping king" he had replaced. Richard had made such an exhibition of himself that people were soon sick of him and refused to take him seriously. Hal is behaving in the same way as Richard. The only person who hasn't seen too much of him is his own father, who weeps at the end of his speech.

Henry's speech is more than 60 lines long, but Hal doesn't interrupt once. (It is hard to imagine Hotspur acting likewise in similar circumstances. We have, remember, just seen how impatient he has been with Owen Glendower.) The Prince listens humbly, and replies simply: "I shall hereafter, my thrice gracious lord, / Be more myself" (emphasizing, of course, that his appearance has not reflected his reality).

But the King goes on again for over 30 lines, without interruption. He compares Hal, unfavorably, with Hotspur. Hotspur is more interested in leading the nation than Hal is, and he is prepared to fight to do so, inspiring older men with his courage and leadership. The King points out that the two of them are the same age, which makes the comparison more acute. (Shakespeare departs from historical truth here. The real-life Hotspur was not only 23 years older than Hal, but older than the King himself.) Hotspur is famous for his courage, "Through all the kingdoms that acknowledge Christ." He is, as Henry hyperbolically puts it, a "Mars in swathling clothes" — that is, like the very god of war himself, and yet still a mere youngster. After valiantly defeating Douglas, Hotspur set him free, and they are now allies in the attempt to "shake the peace and safety of our throne." (Henry's use of the royal "we" emphasizes his dignity and kingship at this point.) The King wonders why he is telling Hal all this; Hal might be dear to him, but he has shown himself to be an enemy. He is so "degenerate" that he will probably join with the rebels against his father.

Prince Hal's reply is magnificent. Here, at last, is the noble character that he promised he would reveal when he spoke his soliloquy at the end of Act I, Scene 2. Hal's response shows dignity and moral purpose, qualities that will flower later in his own heroic kingship, as Henry V, whose story Shakespeare had not yet written. During the present play, these virtues will be seen in his man-to-man fight with Hotspur. Hal promises his father that he will call Hotspur to account. Hal says that he will "redeem" himself, a term with heavy religious significance, calling to mind the sacrifice by which Christ saved mankind from sin. The Elizabethan audience would also have been reminded of the "morality" plays they would have seen, in which virtues and vices battle it out. In the battle for Hal's soul, Good (the call to duty) has triumphed over Evil (the temptation to debauchery). Hal makes a solemn vow to call Hotspur to account.

The King instantly accepts that Hal's reformation is genuine, and says he will give him the authority he needs to carry out his promise. He tells his son to march to Gloucestershire, where their army will assemble in 12 days' time. Twice in this last speech he addresses the Prince as "Harry," which reminds the audience that there is another side to the character known to his low-life friends as "Hal."

Act III, Scene 3

Falstaff avoids paying a debt to the Hostess of the tavern, and the Prince announces that he will make Falstaff an officer in the army.

ACT III, SCENE 3
Eastcheap, the Boar's-head Tavern.

[*Enter* FALSTAFF *and* BARDOLPH.]

Falstaff Bardolph, am I not fallen away vilely since
this last action? do I not bate? do I not dwindle?
Why, my skin hangs about me like an old lady's loose
gown; I am withered like an old apple-john. Well,
I'll repent, and that suddenly, while I am in some   5
liking; I shall be out of heart shortly, and then I shall
have no strength to repent. An I have not forgotten
what the inside of a church is made of, I am a pepper-
corn, a brewer's horse; the inside of a church! Company, villainous company, hath been the spoil of me.   10

Bardolph Sir John, you are so fretful, you cannot
live long.

Falstaff Why, there is it; come sing me a song; make
me merry. I was as virtuously given as a gentleman
need to be; virtuous enough; swore little; diced not   15
above seven times a week; paid money that I bor-
rowed, three or four times; lived well and in good
compass; and now I live out of all order, out of all
compass.

Bardolph Why, you are so fat, Sir John, that you   20
must needs be out of all compass, out of all reason-
able compass, Sir John.

Falstaff Do thou amend thy face, and I'll amend
my life: thou art our admiral, thou bearest the lantern in the poop, but 'tis in the nose of thee; thou art   25
the Knight of the Burning Lamp.

Bardolph Why, Sir John, my face does you no harm.

NOTES

2.   *bate:* decrease, fall off, abate.

4.   *apple-john:* shriveled apple.

7.   *An:* if.

Falstaff No, I'll be sworn; I make as good use of it
as many a man doth of a Death's-head or a memento
mori: I never see thy face but I think upon hell-fire 30
and Dives that lived in purple; for there he is in his
robes, burning, burning. If thou wert any way given
to virtue, I would swear by thy face; my oath should
be 'By this fire, that's God's angel': but thou art altogether given over, and wert indeed, but for the light 35
in thy face, the son of utter darkness. When thou
rannest up Gadshill in the night to catch my horse, if
I did not think thou hadst been an ignis fatuus or a
ball of wildfire, there's no purchase in money. O, thou
art a perpetual triumph, an everlasting bonfirelight! 40
Thou hast saved me a thousand marks in links and
torches, walking with thee in the night betwixt
tavern and tavern: but the sack that thou hast drunk me
would have bought me lights as good cheap at the
dearest chandler's in Europe. I have maintained that 45
salamander of yours with fire any time this two and
thirty years; God reward me for it!

Bardolph 'Sblood, I would my face were in your
stomach!

Falstaff God-a-mercy! so should I be sure to be 50
heartburned.

[*Enter* Hostess.]
How now, Dame Partlet the hen! have you inquired
yet who picked my pocket?

Hostess Why, Sir John, what do you think, Sir John?
do you think I keep thieves in my house? I have 55
searched, I have inquired, so has my husband, man
by man, boy by boy, servant by servant: the tithe of a
hair was never lost in my house before.

Falstaff Ye lie, hostess: Bardolph was shaved and
lost many a hair; and I'll be sworn my pocket was 60
picked. Go to, you are a woman, go.

Hostess Who, I? no; I defy thee: God's light, I was
never called so in mine own house before.

Falstaff Go to, I know you well enough.

29–30. *memento mori:* reminder of death (usually a skull).

31. *Dives:* the wealthy man in the parable of Dives and Lazarus.

38. *ignis fatuus:* fools' fire or will o' the wisp; a light that leads travelers astray in marshes.

41. *links:* flares.

45. *chandler's:* candlestick-maker's.

46. *salamander:* person who likes or can stand a great deal of heat; spirit or other imaginary being that lives in fire (used humorously).

52. *Dame Partlet:* traditional name for hen in fables.

57. *tithe:* tenth part.

Hostess No, Sir John: you do not know me, Sir John.   65
I know you, Sir John; you owe me money, Sir John;
and now you pick a quarrel to beguile me of it: I
bought you a dozen shirts to your back.

Falstaff Dowlas, filthy dowlas: I have given them
away to bakers' wives, and they have made bolters of   70
them.

Hostess Now, as I am a true woman, holland of eight
shillings an ell. You owe money here besides, Sir
John, for your diet and by-drinkings, and money lent
you, four and twenty pound.   75

Falstaff He had his part of it; let him pay.

Hostess He? alas, he is poor; he hath nothing.

Falstaff How! poor? look upon his face; what call
you rich? let them coin his nose, let them coin his
cheeks: I'll not pay a denier. What, will you make a   80
younker of me? shall I not take mine ease in mine
inn but I shall have my pocket picked? I have lost a
sealring of my grandfather's worth forty mark.

Hostess O Jesu, I have heard the prince tell him, I
know not how oft, that that ring was copper!   85

Falstaff How! the prince is a Jack, a neak-cup:
'sblood, an he were here, I would cudgel him like a
dog, if he would say so.

[*Enter the* PRINCE *and* PETO, *marching, and* FALSTAFF
meets them playing on his truncheon like a fife.]
How now, lad! is the wind in that door, i' faith? must
we all march?   90

Bardolph Yea, two and two, Newgate fashion.

Hostess My lord, I pray you, hear me.

Prince What sayst thou, Mistress Quickly? How
doth thy husband? I love him well; he is an honest
man.   95

Hostess Good my lord, hear me.

Falstaff Prithee, let her alone, and list to me.

---

69. *dowlas:* coarse linen.

70. *bolters:* sieves for sifting flour from bran.

72. *holland:* fine linen.

73. *ell:* 45 inches.

80. *denier:* smallest English coin (a tenth of a penny).

81. *younker:* sucker (colloquial).

86. *neak-cup:* sneak-cup, one who steals cups from taverns.

91. *Newgate:* old London prison.

Prince What sayest thou Jack?

Falstaff The other night I fell asleep here behind
the arras and had my pocket picked.

Prince What didst thou lose, Jack?

Falstaff Wilt thou believe me, Hal? three or four
bonds of forty pound a-piece, and a seal-ring of my
grandfather's.

Prince A trifle, some eight-penny matter.

Hostess So I told him, my lord; and I said I heard
your grace say so: and, my lord, he speaks most vilely
of you, like a foul-mouthed man as he is; and said
that he would cudgel you.

Prince What! he did not?

Hostess There's neither faith, truth, nor womanhood
in me else.

Falstaff There's no more faith in thee than in a
stewed prune; nor no more truth in thee than in a
drawn fox; and for womanhood, Maid Marian may
be the deputy's wife of the ward to thee. Go, you
thing, go.

Hostess Say, what thing? what thing?

Falstaff What thing! why, a thing to thank God on.

Hostess I am no thing to thank God on, I would
thou shouldst know it; I am an honest man's wife:
and setting thy knighthood aside, thou art a knave to
call me so.

Prince Thou sayest true, hostess; and he slanders
thee most grossly.

Hostess So he doth you, my lord; and said this
other day you ought him a thousand pound.

Prince Sirrah, do I owe you a thousand pound?

Falstaff A thousand pound, Hal! a million: thy
love is worth a million: thou owest me thy love.

Hostess Nay, my lord, he called you Jack, and said
he would cudgel you.

100

105

110

115

120

125

130

100. *arras:* wall-hanging tapestry.

114. *stewed prune:* prostitute (a "stew" was a brothel).

115. *Maid Marian:* the woman in Robin Hood's gang,
usually played by a lumpish man in the morris
dance referred to here.

Falstaff Did I, Bardolph?

Bardolph Indeed, Sir John, you said so.

Falstaff Yea, if he said my ring was copper.   135

Prince I say 'tis copper: darest thou be as good as
thy word now?

Falstaff Why, Hal, thou know'st, as thou art but
man, I dare; but as thou art prince, I fear thee as
I fear the roaring of the lion's whelp.   140

Prince And why not as the lion?

Falstaff The king himself is to be feared as the
lion: dost thou think I'll fear thee as I fear thy
father? nay, an I do, I pray God my girdle break.

Prince O, if it should! But, sirrah, there's no room   145
for faith, truth, nor honesty in this bosom of thine.
Charge an honest woman with picking thy pocket!
why, thou impudent, embossed rascal, if there were
anything in thy pocket but tavern-reckonings, and
one poor pennyworth of sugar-candy to make thee   150
long-winded, if thy pocket were enriched with any
other injuries but these, I am a villain: and yet you
will stand to it; you will not pocket up wrong: art
thou not ashamed?

Falstaff Dost thou hear, Hal? thou knowest in the   155
state of innocency Adam fell; and what should poor
Jack Falstaff do in the days of villainy? Thou seest
I have more flesh than another man, and therefore
more frailty. You confess then, you picked my pocket?

Prince It appears so by the story.   160

Falstaff Hostess, I forgive thee; go, make ready
breakfast, love thy husband, look to thy servants,
cherish thy guests: thou shalt find me tractable to
any honest reason: thou seest I am pacified still.
Nay, prithee, begone. [*Exit* Hostess.] Now, Hal, to   165
the news at court: for the robbery, lad, how is that
answered?

Prince O, my sweet beef, I must still be good angel
to thee: the money is paid back again.

148. *embossed:* rounded and pressed out (a reference to
Falstaff's fatness).

152. *injuries:* i.e., the things Falstaff pretends were
stolen.

Falstaff O, I do not like that paying back; 'tis a   170
double labour.

Prince I am good friends with my father and may
do any thing.

Falstaff Rob me the exchequer the first thing thou
doest, and do it with unwashed hands too.   175

Bardolph Do, my lord.

Prince I have procured thee, Jack, a charge of foot.

Falstaff I would it had been of horse. Where shall
I find one that can steal well? O for a fine thief, of
the age of two and twenty or thereabouts! I am hein-   180
eously unprovided. Well, God be thanked for these
rebels, they offend none but the virtuous: I laud
them, I praise them.

Prince Bardolph!

Bardolph My lord?   185

Prince Go bear this letter to Lord John of Lancaster, to my brother John; this to my Lord of Westmoreland. [*Exit BARDOLPH.*] Go, Peto, to horse, to
horse; for thou and I have thirty miles to ride yet
ere dinner time. [*Exit* PETO.] Jack, meet me to-   190
morrow in the temple hall at two o'clock in the
afternoon.
There shalt thou know thy charge; and there receive
Money and order for their furniture.
The land is burning; Percy stands on high;   195
And either we or they must lower lie. [*Exit.*]

Falstaff Rare words! brave world! Hostess, my
breakfast, come!
O, I could wish this tavern were my drum! [*Exit.*]

177. *charge of foot:* a company of infantrymen.

191. *temple:* one of the Inns of Court where young
men studied law.

COMMENTARY

Act III, Scene 3 shifts from verse to prose again, marking a very different mood. We move to the Boar's Head Tavern in Eastcheap, where Falstaff is in a melancholy mood. His depression is not surprising, after the prank that was so successfully played upon him. Falstaff feels old and worn out. He speaks of repentance, of turning over a new leaf, but complains that it has been so long since he has seen the inside of a church that he has forgotten what it looks like. The language he uses recalls his obsessions: food and drink. He is "withered like an old apple-john." If he hasn't forgotten what the inside of a church is made of, he is " a pepper-corn, a brewer's horse." Once more, the religious language and references recall the moral significance of Falstaff's actions.

This scene is in marked contrast to the actual repentance that Hal has shown in the previous scene. The Prince is suddenly purposeful; Falstaff, incapable and unwilling to make any effort to change his character. Shakespeare intends to convey these facts clearly, by putting the scenes together like this.

Bardolph insults Falstaff for his fatness; Falstaff likens Bardolph's drink-sozzled nose to a red ship's lantern, in an increasingly fantastic and comic speech, in which Falstaff seems to distract himself from his misery by his increasingly absurd descriptions of Bardolph's face.

The Hostess enters, and Falstaff asks whether she has found out who picked his pocket while he was asleep. Her reply is another example of dramatic irony: "Why, Sir John, do you think I keep thieves in my house?" The audience knows very well that she certainly has a number of them as customers at least. Falstaff picks a quarrel with her, distracting her from the fact that he owes her money. He claims to have been robbed of a valuable signet ring, a family heirloom (dramatic irony again, because the audience knows that nothing more was taken than a few scraps of paper).

The Prince and Peto now enter, and the Hostess appeals to Hal for support, which he gives her. Falstaff insults her by using language that suggests she is a prostitute, and she repeats to Hal some of the insults Falstaff has also leveled against him. Hal admits that he himself picked Falstaff's pocket, which is why he knows that Falstaff is lying about what was in it. Quick-witted as ever, Falstaff "forgives" the Hostess, who leaves, forgetting that she hasn't yet collected the money he owes her.

Hal tells Falstaff that he has paid back the stolen money. He has also arranged for Falstaff to become an officer in the army. The Prince suddenly becomes very business-like and determined, issuing orders to Bardolph and Peto and telling Falstaff to meet him the next day.

The scene has a kind of double-ending. Shakespeare frequently ends scenes with a rhymed couplet, but here there are two. The Prince speaks one grandly and solemnly, before he exits. Falstaff lingers to offer a couplet of his own, calling for his breakfast and lamenting the reality of war. The contrast between the two of them is inescapable.

Notes

KING HENRY IV, PART 1
ACT IV

Vernon *I saw young Harry, with his beaver on,*
His cuisses on his thighs, gallantly arm'd,
Rise from the ground like feather'd Mercury,
And vaulted with such ease into his seat,
As if an angel dropp'd down from the clouds,
To turn and wind a fiery Pegasus
And witch the world with noble horsemanship.

Act IV, Scene 1

Hotspur learns that he will have to face the upcoming battle without many of the troops he had hoped for. Vernon describes the impressive appearance of Prince Hal at the head of the King's army.

ACT IV, SCENE 1
The rebel camp near Shrewsbury.

[*Enter* HOTSPUR, WORCESTER, *and* DOUGLAS.]

Hotspur Well said, my noble Scot: if speaking truth
In this fine age were not thought flattery,
Such attribution should the Douglas have,
As not a soldier of this season's stamp
Should go so general current through the world.   5
By God, I cannot flatter; I do defy
The tongues of soothers; but a braver place
In my heart's love hath no man than yourself:
Nay, task me to my word; approve me, lord.

Douglas Thou art the king of honour: 10
No man so potent breathes upon the ground
But I will beard him.

Hotspur   Do so, and 'tis well.

[*Enter a* Messenger *with letters*.]
What letters hast thou there? — I can but thank you.

Messenger These letters come from your father.

Hotspur Letters from him! why comes he not   15
himself?

Messenger He cannot come, my lord; he is grievous
sick.

Hotspur 'Zounds! how has he the leisure to be sick?
In such a justling time? Who leads his power?
Under whose government come they along?

Messenger His letters bear his mind, not I, my   20
lord.

Worcester I prithee, tell me, doth he keep his bed?

NOTES

3. *attribution:* acclaim.

4–5. *stamp . . . current:* the image is of current coins, the stamp being the picture of a soldier on them.

7. *soothers:* flatterers.

9. *task me:* test or try me.

12. *beard:* challenge.

14. *father:* the Earl of Northumberland.

17. *'Zounds!:* by God's (Christ's) wounds.

18. *justling:* full of clashes (like a joust).
power: army.

Messenger He did, my lord, four days ere I set
    forth;
And at the time of my departure thence
He was much fear'd by his physicians.

Worcester I would the state of time had first been   25
    whole
Ere he by sickness had been visited:
His health was never better worth than now.

Hotspur Sick now! droop now! this sickness doth
    infect
The very life-blood of our enterprise;
'Tis catching hither, even to our camp.   30
He writes me here, that inward sickness —
And that his friends by deputation could not
So soon be drawn, nor did he think it meet
To lay so dangerous and dear a trust
On any soul removed but on his own   35
Yet doth he give us bold advertisement,
That with our small conjunction we should on,
To see how fortune is disposed to us;
For, as he writes, there is no quailing now,
Because the king is certainly possess'd   40
Of all our purposes. What say you to it?

Worcester Your father's sickness is a maim to us.

Hotspur A perilous gash, a very limb lopp'd off
And yet, in faith, it is not; his present want
Seems more than we shall find it: were it good   45
To set the exact wealth of all our states
All at one cast? to set so rich a main
On the nice hazard of one doubtful hour?
It were not good; for therein should we read
The very bottom and the soul of hope,   50
The very list, the very utmost bound
Of all our fortunes.

Douglas   'Faith, and so we should;
Where now remains a sweet reversion:
We may boldly spend upon the hope of what
Is to come in: 55
A comfort of retirement lives in this.

24. *He was:* his life was feared (of).

25. *whole:* the rebellion had been wholly completed.

33. *meet:* appropriate.

36. *advertisement:* advice, counsel (stress falls on the second syllable).

39. *quailing:* cowardly giving up.

40. *possess'd of all our purposes:* knows all our plans.

42. *maim:* crippling disfiguring wound.

47. *main:* prize or reward.

48. *nice hazard:* delicate risk.

    one doubtful hour: the actual battle.

51. *list:* boundary.

    bound: border.

54. *reversion:* expected inheritance.

56. *retirement:* retreat.

Hotspur A rendezvous, a home to fly unto,
　If that the devil and mischance look big
　Upon our affairs.

Worcester But yet I would your father had been　　　60
　　　here.
　The quality and hair of our attempt
　Brooks no division: it will be thought
　By some that know not why he is away,
　That wisdom, loyalty and mere dislike
　Of our proceedings kept the earl from hence　　　65
　And think how such an apprehension
　May turn the tide of fearless faction
　And breed a kind of question in our cause;
　For well you know we of the offering side
　Must keep aloof from strict arbitrement,　　　70
　And stop all sight-holes, every loop from whence
　The eye of reason may pry in upon us:
　This absence of your father's draws a curtain,
　That shows the ignorant a kind of fear
　Before not dreamt of.　　　75

Hotspur　　　　　　You strain too far.
　I rather of his absence make this use:
　It lends a lustre and more great opinion,
　A larger dare to our great enterprise,
　Than if the earl were here; for men must think,
　If we without his help can make a head　　　80
　To push against a kingdom, with his help
　We shall o'erturn it topsy-turvy down.
　Yet all goes well, yet all our joints are whole.

Douglas As heart can think: there is not such a word
　Spoke of in Scotland as this term of fear.　　　85

[*Enter* SIR RICHARD VERNON.]

Hotspur My cousin Vernon! welcome, by my soul.

Vernon Pray God my news be worth a welcome,
　　　lord.
　The Earl of Westmoreland, seven thousand strong,
　Is marching hitherwards; with him Prince John.

Hotspur No harm: what more?　　　90

61.　*hair:* i.e., nature.

62.　*Brooks:* tolerates.

69.　*offering:* challenging.

70.　*arbitrement:* judgment.

71.　*loop:* loophole.

78.　*larger dare:* bigger challenge.

80.　*make a head:* raise an army.

83.　*joints:* limbs.

Vernon   And further, I have learn'd
The king himself in person is set forth,
Or hitherwards intended speedily,
With strong and mighty preparation.

Hotspur He shall be welcome too. Where is his son,
The nimble-footed, madcap Prince of Wales,   95
And his comrades, that daff'd the world aside,
And bid it pass?

Vernon   All furnish'd, all in arms;
All plumed like estridges that wing the wind,
Bated like eagles having lately bathed;
Glittering in golden coats, like images;   100
As full of spirit as the month of May,
And gorgeous as the sun at midsummer;
Sportive as youthful goats, wild as young bulls.
I saw young Harry, with his beaver on,
His cuisses on his thighs, gallantly arm'd,   105
Rise from the ground like feather'd Mercury,
And vaulted with such ease into his seat,
As if an angel dropp'd down from the clouds,
To turn and wind a fiery Pegasus
And witch the world with noble horsemanship.   110

Hotspur No more, no more: worse than the sun in
         March,
This praise doth nourish agues. Let them come;
They come like sacrifices in their trim,
And to the fire-eyed maid of smoky war
All hot and bleeding will we offer them: 115
The mailed Mars shall on his altar sit
Up to the ears in blood. I am on fire
To hear this rich reprisal is so nigh
And yet not ours. Come, let me taste my horse,
Who is to bear me like a thunderbolt   120
Against the bosom of the Prince of Wales:
Harry to Harry shall, hot horse to horse,
Meet and ne'er part till one drop down a corse.
O that Glendower were come!

Vernon   There is more news:
I learn'd in Worcester, as I rode along,   125
He cannot draw his power this fourteen days.

---

98.   *estridges:* ostriches.

104.   *beaver:* face-guard of a helmet.

105.   *cuisses:* thigh-shields or plates.

106.   *Mercury:* messenger of the Roman gods (usually depicted with winged hat and heels).

109.   *wind:* turn.

         Pegasus: the winged horse of classical mythology.

110.   *witch:* bewitch or enchant.

112.   *agues:* fevers.

116.   *mailed:* in (chain-mail) armor.

         Mars: god of war.

118.   *reprisal:* prize, booty.

119.   *taste:* test.

122.   *corse:* corpse.

126.   *draw his power:* muster his soldiers.

Douglas That's the worse tidings that I hear of yet.

Worcester Ay, by my faith, that bears a frosty sound.

Hotspur What may the king's whole battle reach
  unto?

129. *battle:* army.

Vernon To thirty thousand. 130

Hotspur   Forty let it be:
  My father and Glendower being both away,
  The power of us may serve so great a day.
  Come, let us take a muster speedily:
  Doomsday is near; die all, die merrily.

132. *serve:* be sufficient for.

133. *muster:* roll-call, parade.

Douglas Talk not of dying: I am out of fear 135
  Of death or death's hand for this one half-year.

[*Exeunt.*]

COMMENTARY

The sudden seriousness of the last part of the last scene is picked up immediately in Act IV, Scene 1. The setting is the rebel camp; the pace is heating up. Hotspur, Worcester, and Douglas enter, and the play picks up their conversation at the point at which Hotspur is praising the Earl of Douglas to his face, compliments that Douglas returns. Hotspur and the Douglas are like each other in their youthful impetuosity and high sense of honor.

A messenger enters, bearing the news that Hotspur's father, Northumberland, is sick and cannot join them. Hotspur, characteristically, flares up in a curse and a condemnation: "'Zounds! How has he the leisure to be sick?" Worcester more wisely asks for more detail before coming to a judgment: "I prithee, tell me, doth he keep his bed?" Indeed, Northumberland really is ill; his doctors fear for his life. Significantly, the rebel father and son will not be together in the battle, which is the climax of the play. The *royal* father and son, however, will be fighting side by side.

Hotspur reads the letter Northumberland has sent with the messenger, and it advises them to carry on without him. The King must know of their plans by now, and it is too late to go back.

Even though this is terrible news for the rebels, Hotspur talks it up by seeing it as, in one sense, a blessing in disguise, in that not all their forces will be destroyed if they are unlucky enough to suffer defeat. Douglas agrees with him: "A comfort of retirement lives in this." Worcester, however, wiser and older, points out that Northumberland's absence will be taken by some as evidence of division amongst the rebels. They will think that he didn't turn up because he didn't want to.

Hotspur's mind is made up, however, and he tells Worcester "You strain too far." There is another sense in which his father's absence is of benefit: It makes their attempt to overthrow the king a "larger dare," and if they win this battle with much reduced forces, people will have more confidence in supporting them thereafter.

Mercury, winged messenger of the gods.
Musee de Louvre, Paris/SuperStock

dozen or so lines, Vernon paints a glorious picture of the Prince in a catalog of similes drawing up superlative images from nature and supernature. Hal and his comrades are plumed like ostriches, winged like eagles, gorgeous as midsummer sunshine, and as full of life as the month of May.

They are as frisky as goats, as wild as young bulls, and in their shining surcoats they look like the gilded statues of saints. The Prince himself is like Mercury, and like an angel; he leaps unaided onto a horse that is like the mythical creature Pegasus.

All this is too much for Hotspur: "No more, no more," he cries. Instead of being rattled by this description (as the audience must surely think he should be), it makes him all the more impatient — "on fire" — to have to wait to beat King Henry and his son in battle. He is resolved to meet his enemy "Harry to Harry," a phrase that emphasizes the way that Shakespeare has chosen to contrast the two characters.

Shakespeare gives a strong sense here that Hotspur is attempting to provide himself, and the others, with reasons for a course of action he has already decided on, rather than genuinely thinking it through. Douglas agrees with him: He and the Scots have no use for the word "fear."

Sir Richard Vernon arrives, bringing the news that Westmoreland and Prince John are on their way, with an army of seven thousand; the King and his army are coming, too. Hotspur takes this news on the chin, and asks scornfully after the "madcap Prince of Wales."

Vernon's reply brings the rapid pace of the scene to a reflective halt. He describes the figure that Prince Hal cuts in terms of extraordinary poetic intensity. For a

The scene closes with yet more bad news. Vernon adds that he has heard that Owen Glendower can't get his troops together for another fortnight, so he too will miss the battle. Hotspur then asks how many men there are in the King's army: thirty thousand, he is told. Even if it were forty thousand, says Hotspur, we would still win. Only then does Hotspur order his own troops to be counted. Once again, he has spoken first, and thought afterwards. He and Douglas close the scene by expressing their fearless enthusiasm for the fight that is to come; but the audience now knows that the odds are stacked against them.

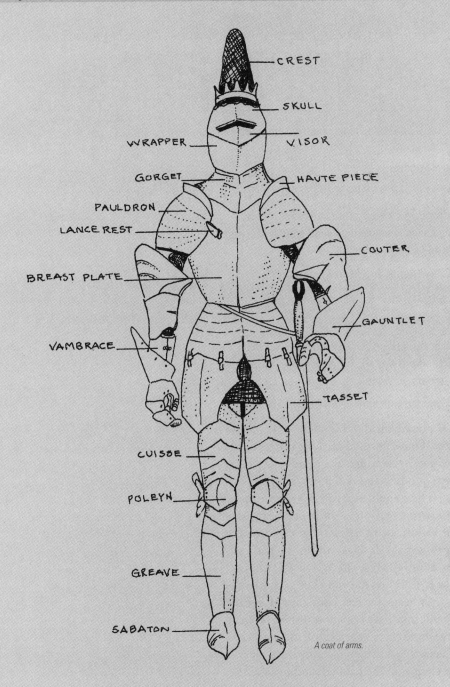

CREST

SKULL

WRAPPER

VISOR

GORGET

HAUTE PIECE

PAULDRON

LANCE REST

COUTER

BREAST PLATE

GAUNTLET

VAMBRACE

TASSET

CUISSE

POLEYN

GREAVE

SABATON

A coat of arms.

Act IV, Scene 2

Falstaff explains how his dishonest recruiting policy has left him with a troop of men who will be no good in a fight.

ACT IV, SCENE 2
A public road near Coventry.

[*Enter* FALSTAFF *and* BARDOLPH.]

Falstaff Bardolph, get thee before to Coventry; fill
me a bottle of sack: our soldiers shall march through;
we'll to Sutton Co'fil' tonight.

Bardolph Will you give me money, captain?

Falstaff Lay out, lay out.   5

Bardolph This bottle makes an angel.

Falstaff An if it do, take if for thy labour; and if it
make twenty, take them all, I'll answer the coinage.
Bid my lieutenant Peto meet me at town's end.

Bardolph I will, captain: farewell. [*Exit.*]   10

Falstaff If I be not ashamed of my soldiers, I am a
soused gurnet. I have misused the king's press dam-
nably. I have got, in exchange of a hundred and fifty
soldiers, three hundred and odd pounds. I press me
none but good householders, yeomen's sons; inquire   15
me out contracted bachelors, such as had been asked
twice on the banns; such a commodity of warm slaves,
as had as lieve hear the devil as a drum; such as fear
the report of a caliver worse that a struck fowl or a
hurt wild-duck. I pressed me none but such toasts-   20
and-butter, with hearts in their bodies no bigger than
pins' heads, and they have bought out their services;
and now my whole charge consists of ancients, cor-
porals, lieutenants, gentlemen of companies, slaves
as ragged as Lazarus in the painted cloth, where the   25
glutton's dogs licked his sores; and such as indeed
were never soldiers, but discarded unjust serving-
men, younger sons to younger brothers, revolted
tapsters and ostlers trade-fallen, the cankers of a calm

NOTES

1.   *get thee before:* go on ahead.

3.   *Sutton Co' fil':* Sutton Coldfield (place).

5.   *Lay out:* spend your money.

6.   *angel:* gold coin.

12.   *soused gurnet:* pickled fish.

      king's press: power to conscript in the king's name.

16.   *contracted bachelors:* young men who are engaged to be married.

17.   *warm:* i.e., comfort-loving.

18.   *lieve:* gladly.

19.   *caliver:* light kind of musket.

20.   *toasts-and-butter:* self-indulgent men.

22.   *bought out their services:* purchased their release from conscription.

23.   *ancients:* a rank in the army under lieutenant; a standard-bearer.

world and a long peace, ten times more dishonourable   30
ragged than an old faced ancient: and such have I,
to fill up the rooms of them that have bought out
their services, that you would think that I had a hundred and fifty tattered prodigals lately come from
swine-keeping, from eating draff and husks. A mad   35
fellow met me on the way and told me I had unloaded
all the gibbets and pressed the dead bodies. No eye
hath seen such scarecrows. I'll not march through
Coventry with them, that's flat: nay, and the villains
march wide betwixt the legs, as if they had gyves on;   40
for indeed I had the most of them out of prison.
There's but a shirt and a half in all my company;
and the half shirt is two napkins tacked together and
thrown over the shoulders like an herald's coat without sleeves; and the shirt, to say the truth, stolen   45
from my host at St. Alban's, or the red-nose inn-
keeper of Daventry. But that's all one; they'll find
linen enough on every hedge.

[*Enter the* PRINCE *and* WESTMORELAND.]

Prince How now, blown Jack! how now, quilt!

Falstaff What, Hal! how now, mad wag! what a   50
Devil dost thou in Warwickshire? My good Lord of
Westmoreland, I cry you mercy: I thought your hon-
our had already been at Shrewsbury.

Westmoreland Faith, Sir John, 'tis more than time
that I were there, and you too; but my powers are   55
there already. The king, I can tell you, looks for us
all: we must away all night.

Falstaff Tut, never fear me: I am as vigilant as a
cat to steal cream.

Prince I think, to steal cream indeed, for thy theft   60
hath already made thee butter. But tell me, Jack,
whose fellows are these that come after?

Falstaff Mine, Hal, mine.

Prince I did never see such pitiful rascals

Falstaff Tut, tut; good enough to toss; food for   65
powder, food for powder; they'll fill a pit as well as
better: tush man, mortal men, mortal men

---

35. *draff:* swill.

37. *gibbets:* gallows.
     pressed: conscripted.

40. *gyves:* fetters, shackles.

42. *but a:* only one.

48. *linen:* shirts that are placed on hedges to dry after
     having been washed.

49. *quilt:* padded coat (humorously applied to a fat
     person).

65. *toss:* i.e., on the end of a pike.

65–66. *food for powder:* food for gunpowder;
        "canon-fodder."

Westmoreland Ay, but, Sir John, methinks they are exceeding poor and bare, too beggarly.

Falstaff 'Faith, for their poverty, I know not where   70
they had that; and for their bareness, I am sure they
never learned that of me.

Prince No, I'll be sworn; unless you call three fin-
gers on the ribs bare. But, sirrah, make haste: Percy
is already in the field.   75

Falstaff What, is the king encamped?

Westmoreland He is, Sir John: I fear we shall stay
too long.

Falstaff Well,
To the latter end of a fray and the beginning of a   80
     feast
Fits a dull fighter and keen guest. [*Exeunt.*]

COMMENTARY

Act IV, Scene 2 shifts the action back to the low-life characters — and back to prose. Falstaff and his companions are now in the King's army, but even though they are in uniform, their talk is not of war, but of drink. Falstaff, who has been made a captain by Prince Hal, sends Bardolph ahead to Coventry to get him a bottle of sack. When he has gone, Falstaff soliloquizes (in prose) on how he has used his commission to make money. He has purposely conscripted men whom he knew would have good reason to want to buy their way out, and he has made over three hundred pounds in so doing. (Establishing a modern value for such a figure is impossible, but it is a very large amount of money, indeed.) Having allowed the best men to pay to escape conscription, Falstaff is left with a collection of rogues, tramps, and misfits that a passerby said looked like an army of men cut down from the gibbets where executed criminals were displayed. They haven't even clothes for their backs; they'll have to steal washing laid out to dry as they make their way to battle.

Falstaff is surprised by the arrival of Prince Hal, who tells him that he "never did see such pitiful rascals." Falstaff says, with astonishing cynicism, that they are good enough for cannon fodder and will fill a grave as well as their betters would; but the conversation is cut short by Prince Hal's need for haste. The time for the battle is getting very close.

Falstaff's contempt for the men he has recruited is expressed in his characteristically comically exaggerated language, but our laughter rings hollow as we realize that he is speaking of matters of life and death. The couplet with which Falstaff closes the scene picks up the Prince's reference to food, the likes of which follow Sir John throughout the play. He is looking forward to the end of the battle so that he can enjoy the victory feast that will follow it.

The vitality and energy that characterize Falstaff's speech continue to impress us, but they are qualities that seem increasingly at odds with the moral seriousness of the circumstances in which he now finds himself. It is as if Shakespeare is encouraging us to qualify our admiration for him at this point, and to think of him as a rounded character (in more than one sense!) as the play moves to its conclusion. Life, even for great characters like Sir John Falstaff, is not always simple.

Act IV, Scene 3

The rebels argue about whether to attack now or later. The King sends a messenger to offer a chance to talk of peace. Hotspur says he will send his answer with Worcester in the morning.

ACT IV, SCENE 3
The rebel camp near Shrewsbury.

[*Enter* HOTSPUR, WORCESTER, DOUGLAS, *and*
   VERNON.]

Hotspur We'll fight with him to-night.

Worcester   It may not be.

Douglas You give him then advantage.

Vernon   Not a whit.

Hotspur Why say you so? looks he not for supply?

Vernon So do we.

Hotspur   His is certain, ours is doubtful.

Worcester Good cousin, be advised; stir not to-night.   5

Vernon Do not, my lord.

Douglas   You do not counsel well:
  You speak it out of fear and cold heart.

Vernon Do me no slander, Douglas: by my life,
  And I dare well maintain it with my life,
  If well-respected honour bid me on,   10
  I hold as little counsel with weak fear
  As you, my lord, or any Scot that this day lives:
  Let it be seen to-morrow in the battle
  Which of us fears.

Douglas   Yea, or to-night.

Vernon   Content.

Hotspur To-night, say I.   15

Vernon Come, come, it may not be. I wonder much
  Being men of such great leading as you are,
  That you forsee not what impediments
  Drag back our expedition: certain horse

NOTES

3.   *supply:* supplies of horses, equipment, food, and men.

Of my cousin Vernon's are not yet come up: 20
Your uncle Worcester's horse came but to-day;
And now their pride and mettle is asleep,   **22.** *mettle:* spirit.
Their courage with hard labour tame and dull,
That not a horse is half the half of himself.

Hotspur So are the horses of the enemy   25
In general, journey-bated and brought low: **26.** *journey-bated:* tired out from traveling.
The better part of ours are full of rest.

Worcester The number of the king exceedeth ours:
For God's sake, cousin, stay till all come in.

[*The trumpet sounds a parley.*]

[*Enter* SIR WALTER BLUNT.]

Blunt I come with gracious offers from the king   30
If you vouchsafe me hearing and respect.

Hotspur Welcome, Sir Walter Blunt; and would to
    God
You were of our determination!   **33.** *determination:* persuasion or beliefs.
Some of us love you well; and even those some
Envy your great deservings and good name,   35
Because you are not of our quality,   **36.** *quality:* side.
But stand against us like an enemy.

Blunt And God defend but still I should stand so,
So long as out of limit and true rule
You stand against anointed majesty.   40   **40.** *anointed majesty:* reference to the sacred ritual of coronation and the divine right of duly anointed monarchs.
But to my charge. The king hath sent to know
The nature of your griefs, and whereupon   **42.** *whereupon:* on what grounds, why.
You conjure from the breast of civil peace   **43.** *conjure:* evoke.
Such bold hostility, teaching his duteous land
Audacious cruelty. If that the king   45
Have any way your good deserts forgot,   **46.** *forgot:* forgotten.
Which he confesseth to be manifold,
He bids you name your griefs; and with all speed
You shall have your desires with interest
And pardon absolute for yourself and these   50
Herein misled by your suggestion.

Hotspur The king is kind; and well we know the
    king
Knows at what time to promise, when to pay.

My father and my uncle and myself
Did give him that same royalty he wears;   55
And when he was not six and twenty strong,
Sick in the world's regard, wretched and low,
A poor unminded outlaw sneaking home,
My father gave him welcome to the shore;
And when he heard him swear and vow to God   60
He came but to be Duke of Lancaster,
To sue his livery and beg his peace,
With tears of innocency and terms of zeal,
My father, in kind heart and pity moved,
Swore him assistance and perform'd it too.   65
Now when the lords and barons of the realm
Perceived Northumberland did lean to him,
The more and less came in with cap and knee;
Met him in boroughs, cities, villages,
Attended him on bridges, stood in lanes,   70
Laid gifts before him, proffer'd him their oaths,
Gave him their heirs as pages, follow'd him
Even at the heels in golden multitudes.
He presently, as greatness knows itself,
Steps me a little higher than his vow   75
Made to my father, while his blood was poor,
Upon the naked shore at Ravenspurgh;
And now, forsooth, takes on him to reform
Some certain edicts and some strait decrees
That lie too heavy on the commonwealth,   80
Cries out upon abuses, seems to weep
Over his country's wrongs; and by this face,
This seeming brow of justice, did he win
The hearts of all that he did angle for;
Proceeded further; cut me off the heads   85
Of all the favourites that the absent king
In deputation left behind him here,
When he was personal in the Irish war.

Blunt Tut, I came not to hear this.

Hotspur   Then to the point.
In short time after, he deposed the king;   90
Soon after that, deprived him of his life;
And in the neck of that, task'd the whole state
To make that worse, suffered his kinsman March,

---

54. *father:* Earl of Northumberland.

uncle: Earl of Worcester.

myself: Harry Percy (Hotspur).

55. *him:* Henry Bolingbroke, then Duke of Lancaster.

62. *sue his livery:* sue (in court) for his right to the Dukedom.

67. *lean to him:* incline to his cause.

76. *blood was poor:* was not royal.

79. *strait:* strict.

84. *angle:* fish (for).

88. *was personal in:* attended in person.

92. *in the neck of:* straight after.

Who is, if every owner were well placed,
Indeed his king, to be engaged in Wales,   95
There without ransom to lie forfeited;
Disgraced me in my happy victories,
Sought to entrap me by intelligence;
Rated mine uncle from the council-board;
In rage dismissed my father from the court;   100
Broke oath on oath, committed wrong on wrong,
And in conclusion drove us to seek out
This head of safety; and withal to pry
Into his title, the which we find
Too indirect for long continuance.   105

Blunt Shall I return this answer to the king?

Hotspur Not so, Sir Walter: we'll withdraw awhile.
Go to the king; and let there be impawn'd
Some surety for a safe return again,
And in the morning early shall my uncle   110
Bring him our purposes; and so farewell.

Blunt I would you would accept of grace and love.

Hotspur And may be so we shall.

Blunt   Pray God you do. [*Exeunt.*]

99.   *Rated:* berated, drove out.
        council-board: Council of State.

103.   *head of safety:* self-defensive army.
        withal: additionally.

104.   *title:* claim to the throne based on line of descent.

108.   *impawn'd:* pledged.

111.   *purposes:* proposals.

COMMENTARY

Act IV, Scene 3 takes place once more with the rebels, and Hotspur begins the scene with a decision: "We'll fight with him tonight." Again, the decision comes before the discussion. Hotspur is as impetuous as ever. Vernon and Worcester are against it: The army is not ready to fight. Douglas, as eager for battle and for glory as Hotspur, dismisses their advice as cowardice.

Vernon and Worcester list the reasons for delay: Some of their troops haven't yet arrived; many of those who have are exhausted; in any case, they are outnumbered.

The argument, which does not bode well for the rebels' success in the coming battle, is interrupted by a trumpet-call to a parley. Sir Walter Blunt, the King's messenger, arrives. The King has asked the rebels to tell him of their grievances. If they are his fault, which he confesses they might well be, he promises to make amends and give them and their followers full pardons.

Hotspur will have none of it. Promises are one thing; carrying them out, another. He recounts what has driven them to rebellion. The Percy clan stood by Bolingbroke when he returned from exile, but he then wheedled his way into people's good opinions, got rid of the supporters of King Richard II while he was away fighting in Ireland, and had Richard deposed and murdered. Moreover, Bolingbroke refused to ransom Mortimer, dishonored and spied on Hotspur, sacked his uncle from the council, dismissed his father from court, and broke promise after promise. All this forced them to form an army to stand up for themselves. Moreover, they believe that King Henry has a poor claim to the throne. The climax of Hotspur's complaint is a rhetorically shaped sentence some 15 lines long, which would seem to bring him to the point of sending Blunt back with a resounding "no" to the King's offer; and yet, most uncharacteristically, Hotspur asks for time (that night) to consider it. It is as if Hotspur sees himself at the very brink of the conflict that he has been so purposefully seeking, and he feels he must, just this once, pause for thought, and take a breath before charging into battle. By making him do this, Shakespeare skillfully maintains the tension that will be unleashed when the fighting begins.

Act IV, Scene 4

The Archbishop of York sends letters preparing for the possibility that his fellow rebels will lose the battle.

ACT IV, SCENE 4
York, the Archbishop's palace.

[*Enter the* ARCHBISHOP OF YORK *and* SIR MICHAEL.]

Archbishop Hie, good Sir Michael; bear this sealed
　　brief
With winged haste to the lord marshal;
This to my cousin Scroop, and all the rest
To whom they are directed. If you knew
How much they do import, you would make haste.　　5

Sir Michael My good lord,
I guess their tenour.

Archbishop　　　　　Like enough you do
To-morrow, good Sir Michael, is a day
Wherein the fortune of ten thousand men
Must bide the touch; for, sir, at Shrewsbury,　　10
As I am truly given to understand,
The king with mighty and quick-raised power
Meets with Lord Harry: and, I fear, Sir Michael,
What with the sickness of Northumberland,
Whose power was in the first proportion,　　15
And what with Owen Glendower's absence thence,
Who with them was a rated sinew too
And comes not in, o'er-ruled by prophecies,
I fear the power of Percy is too weak
To wage an instant trial with the king.　　20

Sir Michael Why, my good lord, you need not fear;
There is Douglas and Lord Mortimer.

Archbishop No, Mortimer is not there.

Sir Michael But there is Mordake, Vernon, Lord
　　Harry Percy
And there is my Lord of Worcester and a head　　25
Of gallant warriors, noble gentlemen.

NOTES

1.　*Hie:* hasten.

　　brief: letter.

2.　*lord marshal:* the earl marshal of England, the Duke of Norfolk.

7.　*tenour:* import.

10.　*bide the touch:* be tested.

12.　*power:* army.

15.　*in the first proportion:* i.e., the largest.

17.　*rated sinew:* esteemed source of strength.

Archbishop And so there is: but yet the king hath
    drawn
The special head of all the land together:
The Prince of Wales, Lord John of Lancaster,
The noble Westmoreland and warlike Blunt;   30
And many moe corrivals and dear men
Of estimation and command in arms.

Sir Michael Doubt not, my lord, they shall be well
    opposed.

Archbishop I hope no less, yet needful 'tis to fear;
And, to prevent the worst, Sir Michael, speed: 35
For if Lord Percy thrive not, ere the king
Dismiss his power, he means to visit us,
For he hath heard of our confederacy,
And 'tis but wisdom to make strong against him:
Therefore make haste. I must go write again   40
To other friends; and so farewell, Sir Michael.

[*Exeunt.*]

28.   *special head:* elite force.

31.   *moe corrivals:* more fellows-at-arms.

COMMENTARY

This scene is very often cut when the play is performed, because it does little more than underline facts that the audience already knows, emphasizing the odds that the rebels will shortly face in battle. The scene does, however, remind us of the involvement of the Archbishop of York in the plot, and provides a link to the events of Shakespeare's next play in the sequence, *King Henry IV, Part 2.*

The Archbishop orders Sir Michael to take messages to various rebel sympathizers, so that if the battle is lost, they will be prepared for the consequences. He is sure that the King knows of his complicity: "he hath heard of our confederacy." The Archbishop's anxiety contributes to the tension as they are on the very brink of the battle, and it underlines the fact that those rebels who will actually take part in the fighting are underdogs, which inevitably engages at least a little of our sympathy.

Archbishop's mitre.
Musee de Louvre, Paris/SuperStock

Notes

KING HENRY IV, PART 1
ACT V

King *Rebellion in this land shall lose his sway,*
Meeting the check of such another day:
And since this business so fair is done,
Let us not leave till all our own be won.

Act V, Scene 1

Worcester and Vernon go to the King for a last parley before the battle. The King asks them to carry an offer of peace to Hotspur and his army if they will accept his authority. Falstaff speaks scornfully of the idea of honor.

ACT V, SCENE 1
The King's camp near Shrewsbury.

[*Enter the* KING, PRINCE OF WALES, LORD JOHN OF
　　LANCASTER, EARL OF WESTMORELAND, SIR
　　WALTER BLUNT, *and* FALSTAFF.]

King How bloodily the sun begins to peer
　Above yon husky hill! the day looks pale
　At his distemperature.

Prince　　　　　　　　The southern wind
　Doth play the trumpet to his purposes,
　And by his hollow whistling in the leaves　　　　　　5
　Foretells a tempest and a blustering day.

King Then with the losers let it sympathise,
　For nothing can seem foul to those that win.

[*The trumpet sounds.*]

[*Enter* WORCESTER *and* VERNON.]
　How now, my lord of Worcester! 'tis not well
　That you and I should meet upon such terms　　　　　10
　As now we meet. You have deceived our trust
　And made us doff our easy robes of peace,
　To crush our old limbs in ungentle steel:
　This is not well, my lord, this is not well.
　What say you to it? Will you again unknit　　　　　　15
　This churlish knot of all-abhorred war?
　And move in that obedient orb again
　Where you did give a fair and natural light,
　And be no more an exhaled meteor,
　A prodigy of fear and a portent　　　　　　　　　20
　Of broached mischief to the unborn times?

Worcester Hear me, my liege:
　For mine own part, I could be well content
　To entertain the lag-end of my life

NOTES

2.　*husky:* bushy.

3.　*distemperature:* sickness.

10.　*such terms:* as representatives of opposing forces.

12.　*doff:* discard or take off.

13.　*ungentle steel:* uncomfortable armor.

15.　*unknit:* unravel or take to pieces.

20.　*prodigy of fear:* evil omen.

With quiet hours; for I do protest,   25
I have not sought the day of this dislike.

King You have not sought it! how comes it, then?

Falstaff Rebellion lay in his way, and he found it.

Prince Peace, chewet, peace!

Worcester It pleased your majesty to turn your   30
  looks
Of favour from myself and all our house;
And yet I must remember you, my lord,
We were the first and dearest of your friends.
For you my staff of office did I break
In Richard's time; and posted day and night   35
To meet you on the way, and kiss your hand,
When yet you were in place and in account
Nothing so strong and fortunate as I.
It was myself, my brother and his son,
That brought you home and boldly did outdare   40
The dangers of the time. You swore to us,
And you did swear that oath at Doncaster,
That you did nothing purpose 'gainst the state;
Nor claim no further than your new-fall'n right,
The seat of Gaunt, dukedom of Lancaster;   45
To this we swore our aid. But in short space
It rain'd down fortune showering on your head;
And such a flood of greatness fell on you
What with our help, what with the absent king,
What with the injuries of a wanton time,   50
The seeming sufferances that you had borne,
And the contrarious winds that held the king
So long in his unlucky Irish wars
That all in England did repute him dead:
And from this swarm of fair advantages   55
You took occasion to be quickly woo'd
To gripe the general sway into your hand;
Forgot your oath to us at Doncaster;
And being fed by us you used us so
As that ungentle gull, the cuckoo's bird   60
Useth the sparrow; did oppress our nest;
Grew by our feeding to so great a bulk
That even our love durst not come near your sight

29. *chewet:* chatterer.

32. *remember:* remind.

35. *posted:* rode post-haste.

For fear of swallowing; but with nimble wing
We were enforced, for safety sake, to fly   65
Out of your sight and raise this present head
Whereby we stand opposed by such means
As you yourself have forged against yourself
By unkind usage, dangerous countenance,
And violation of all faith and troth   70
Sworn to us in your younger enterprise.

King These things indeed you have articulate,
Proclaim'd at market-crosses, read in churches,
To face the garment of rebellion
With some fine colour that may please the eye   75
Of fickle changelings and poor discontents,
Which gape and rub the elbow at the news
Of hurlyburly innovation:
And never yet did insurrection want
Such water-colours to impaint his cause;   80
Nor moody beggars, starving for a time
Of pellmell havoc and confusion.

Prince In both your armies there is many a soul
Shall pay full dearly for this encounter,
If once they join in trial. Tell your nephew,   85
The Prince of Wales doth join with all the world
In praise of Henry Percy: by my hopes,
This present enterprise set off his head,
I do not think a braver gentleman,
More active-valiant or more valiant-young,   90
More daring or more bold, is now alive
To grace this latter age with noble deeds.
For my part, I may speak it to my shame,
I have a truant been to chivalry;
And so I hear he doth account me too;   95
Yet this before my father's majesty —
I am content that he shall take the odds
Of his great name and estimation,
And will, to save the blood on either side,
Try fortune with him in a single fight.   100

King And, Prince of Wales, so dare we venture thee,
Albeit considerations infinite
Do make against it. No, good Worcester, no,
We love our people well; even those we love

69.   *unkind:* unnatural.

72.   *articulate:* set out in clear terms.

79.   *want:* lack.

94.   *truant:* absentee.

That are misled upon your cousin's part; 105
And, will they take the offer of our grace,
Both he and they and you, yea, every man
Shall be my friend again and I'll be his,
So tell your cousin, and bring me word
What he will do: but if he will not yield, 110
Rebuke and dread correction wait on us,
And they shall do their office. So, be gone;
We will not now be troubled with reply:
We offer fair; take it advisedly.

[*Exeunt* WORCESTER *and* VERNON.]

Prince It will not be accepted, on my life: 115
The Douglas and the Hotspur both together
Are confident against the world in arms.

King Hence, therefore, every leader to his charge:
For, on their answer, will we set on them:
And God befriend us, as our cause is just! 120

[*Exeunt all but the* PRINCE OF WALES *and* FALSTAFF.]

Falstaff Hal, if thou see me down in the battle and
bestride me, so; 'tis a point of friendship.

Prince Nothing but a colossus can do thee that
friendship. Say thy prayers, and farewell.

Falstaff I would 'twere bed-time, Hal, and all well. 125

Prince Why, thou owest God a death. [*Exit.*]

Falstaff 'T is not due yet; I would be loath to pay
him before his day. What need I be so forward with
him that calls not on me? Well, 'tis no matter;
honour pricks me on. Yea, but how if honour prick 130
me off when I come on? how then? Can honour set to a
leg? no: or an arm? no: or take away the grief of a
wound? no. Honour hath no skill in surgery, then?
no. What is honour? a word. What is in that word honour? what is that honour? air. A trim reckoning! 135
Who hath it? he that died o' Wednesday. Doth he feel
it? no. Doth he hear it? no. 'Tis insensible, then. Yea,
to the dead. But will it not live with the living? no.
Why? detraction will not suffer it. Therefore I'll
none of it. Honour is a mere scutcheon; and so ends 140
my catechism. [*Exeunt.*]

109. *cousin:* kinsman.

121. *bestride:* stand over, one leg on each side.

123. *colossus:* gigantic statue (like the one that reputedly bestrode the bay outside Rhodes).

130–131. *prick me off:* tick me off on a list.

131. *set to:* set (bones).

135. *A trim reckoning:* "A fine account that is!"

140. *scutcheon:* simple shield on a coat of arms such as is displayed at funerals.

141. *catechism:* series of doctrinal questions and answers to be learned by heart.

COMMENTARY

The last act begins with the dawn of the day of the battle. Shakespeare starts the action in the King's camp. King Henry and the Prince see the sun rise "bloodily" and believe that the "hollow whistling" of the wind "Foretells a tempest and a blustering day." These observations instantly create a heavy and threatening mood. Nature is ominously reflecting the violence and bloodshed that are to come. This momentary musing is abruptly interrupted by the sound of a trumpet: The rebels' representatives, Worcester and Vernon, have arrived.

The King greets Worcester sternly, and speaks to him in language that is richly poetic. This language not only vividly suggests the disorder that rebellion brings, but conveys a sense of Henry's king-like dignity. He uses the royal "we": "You have deceived our trust." He invites Worcester to return to obedience and once more shine like a "fair and *natural* light, / And be no more an exhaled meteor." These contrasting images emphasize the consequences of rebellion: The very natural order of things is overturned. (Meteors were then regarded as omens of disorder.)

Worcester replies by claiming that this war is not of his making. Challenged to justify himself, he retells the story of how he has been driven to rebel against the King. Worcester had been among the first to welcome Henry back from exile, supporting him in his claim to the Dukedom of Lancaster. Henry had sworn that he "did nothing purpose 'gainst the state," an oath he later "forgot" as he had risen in power and influence during the rightful King Richard's absence.

Worcester's imagery is more down-to-earth than the King's: He describes the way that he and his family and friends were used in the same way that a cuckoo uses a sparrow's nest, putting in a chick, which quickly becomes so big that the others are driven out. The picture is a vivid one, but it contrasts with the grander images used by the King. Compared with Henry's talk of orbs and meteors, things that affect the whole state, Worcester's language seems petty and personal. It emphasizes the pain he and his friends have suffered as individuals. He sums up Henry's offences as "unkind usage, dangerous countenance, / And violation of all faith and troth / Sworn to *us* in your younger enterprise."

The Prince then speaks up. The coming battle will cost the lives of "many a soul." He valiantly offers to settle the issue by single combat with Hotspur, whom he praises for his bravery and nobility. He admits that he has himself " a truant been to chivalry" in the past, but offers to put this right now "to save the blood on either side." This is the reformed Hal speaking, a total contrast with the characteristics he has shown previously in the tavern scenes and in his low-life escapades. The reformed Hal is also utterly unlike the selfish Falstaff, who has little regard for the lives of the men he now commands.

The King asks Worcester to tell the rebels that he still extends the hand of peace if they will take it. His language again emphasizes responsible kingship. He uses the royal "we," expressing his responsibility to all of his subjects: "*We* love *our* people well" — even those who have been led astray. If the rebels don't accept his "grace," they must face the consequences. "Grace" is a word with religious overtones: It suggests the goodness of God, and its use here indicates that God is on the side of the rightly ruling King, a claim that Henry makes explicitly a few lines later. He orders his troops to prepare to fight.

Now that the battle seems inevitable, Falstaff asks the Prince to stand over him should he fall in the fighting, and Hal jokingly points out how difficult that would be, given his size.

Falstaff is left alone on the stage, and makes an important speech, which stops the rapidly accelerating pace of the play for a moment, and invites us to think about the meaning of honor — something that will be fiercely fought for shortly, and which is a key theme of the play. Honor is a word, nothing more than air; to die for it is foolish. Falstaff won't be doing so, if he can help it.

Falstaff's cynical attitude is in direct contrast to that of the heroic figures, Hal and Hotspur, who will shortly be facing each other in honorable combat. This situation recalls that when powerful rulers engage in battle, it is ordinary folk who have to pay the price in order for their honor to be satisfied. All the major themes of the play now weave together as it draws to a climax. Ideas of kingship, honor, duty, responsibility, loyalty, good and evil, appearance and reality, and the relationship between fathers and sons all arise quickly now as the play approaches its resolution.

Act V, Scene 2

Worcester decides that he and Vernon should not pass on the King's generous offer of peace, in case it is accepted. The trumpets sound the beginning of the battle.

ACT V, SCENE 2
The rebel camp.

[*Enter* WORCESTER *and* VERNON.]

Worcester O, no, my nephew must not know, Sir
    Richard,
The liberal and kind offer of the king.

Vernon 'Twere best he did.

Worcester   Then are we all undone.
It is not possible, it cannot be,
The king should keep his word in loving us;   5
He will suspect us still and find a time
To punish this offence in other faults;
Suspicion all our lives shall be stuck full of eyes;
For treason is but trusted like the fox,
Who, ne'er so tame, so cherish'd, and lock'd up,   10
Will have a wild trick of his ancestors.
Look how we can, or sad or merrily,
Interpretation will misquote our looks,
And we shall feed like oxen at a stall,
The better cherish'd still the nearer death.   15
My nephew's trespass may be well forgot;
It hath the excuse of youth and heat of blood,
And an adopted name of privilege,
A hare-brain'd Hotspur, govern'd by a spleen:
All his offences live upon my head   20
And on his father's; we did train him on,
And, his corruption being ta'en from us,
We, as the spring of all, shall pay for all.
Therefore, good cousin, let not Harry know
In any case, the offer of the king.   25

Vernon Deliver what you will; I'll say 'tis so.
Here comes your cousin.

[*Enter* HOTSPUR *and* DOUGLAS.]

NOTES

3.   *undone:* ruined.

7.   *in:* along with.

8.   *stuck full of eyes:* i.e., always looking at us.

10.   *never so:* however.

11.   *trick:* characteristic.

19.   *a spleen:* hot-headedness.

23.   *spring:* fount, origin.

Hotspur My uncle is return'd:
　Deliver up my Lord of Westmoreland.
　Uncle, what news?　　　　　　　　　　　　　　　　30

Worcester The king will bid you battle presently.

Douglas Defy him by the Lord of Westmoreland.

Hotspur Lord Douglas, go you and tell him so.

Douglas Marry, and shall, and very willingly.

[*Exeunt.*]

Worcester There is no seeming mercy in the king.　　35

Hotspur Did you beg any? God forbid.

Worcester I told him gently of our grievances,
　Of his oath-breaking; which he mended thus,
　By now forswearing that he is forsworn:
　He calls us rebels, traitors; and will scourge　　40
　With haughty arms this hateful name in us.

[*Re-enter* DOUGLAS.]

Douglas Arm, gentlemen; to arms! for I have
　　　thrown
　A brave defiance in King Henry's teeth,
　And Westmoreland, that was engaged, did bear it;
　Which cannot choose but bring him quickly on.　　45

Worcester The Prince of Wales stepp'd forth be-
　　　fore the king,
　And, nephew, challenged you to single fight.

Hotspur O, would the quarrel lay upon our heads,
　And that no man might draw short breath to-day
　But I and Harry Monmouth! Tell me, tell me,　　50
　How show'd his tasking? seem'd it in contempt?

Vernon No, by my soul; I never in my life
　Did hear a challenge urged more modestly,
　Unless a brother should a brother dare
　To gentle exercise and proof of arms.　　55
　He gave you all the duties of a man:
　Trimm'd up your praises with a princely tongue,
　Spoke your deservings like a chronicle,
　Making you ever better than his praise
　By still dispraising praise valued with you;　　60

34. *Marry:* by (the Virgin) Mary.

and shall: I will.

39. *foreswearing:* swearing falsely.

56. *all the duties of a man:* all the respect manhood deserves.

60. *dispraising praise valued with you:* saying that you were better than words of praise could express.

And, which became him like a prince indeed,
He made a blushing cital of himself;
And chid his truant youth with such a grace
As if he master'd there a double spirit
Of teaching and of learning instantly. 65
There did he pause: but let me tell the world,
If he outlive the envy of this day,
England did never owe so sweet a hope,
So much misconstrued in his wantonness.

Hotspur Cousin, I think thou art enamoured 70
On his follies: never did I hear
Of any prince so wild a libertine.
But be he as he will, yet once ere night
I will embrace him with a soldier's arm,
That he shall shrink under my courtesy. 75
Arm, arm with speed: and, fellows, soldiers, friends,
Better consider what you have to do
Than I, that have not well the gift of tongue,
Can lift your blood up with persuasion.

[*Enter a* Messenger.]

Messenger My lord, here are letters for you. 80

Hotspur I cannot read them now.
O gentlemen, the time of life is short!
To spend that shortness basely were too long,
If life did ride upon a dial's point,
Still ending at the arrival of an hour. 85
An if we live, we live to tread on kings;
If die, brave death, when princes die with us!
Now, for our consciences, the arms are fair,
When the intent of bearing them is just.

[*Enter another* Messenger.]

Messenger My lord, prepare; the king comes on 90
    apace.

Hotspur I thank him, that he cuts me from my tale,
For I profess not talking; only this —
Let each man do his best: and here draw I
A sword, whose temper I intend to stain
With the best blood that I can meet withal 95
In the adventure of this perilous day.

62. *cital:* reproach.

70. *enamoured on:* in love with.

72. *libertine:* person without moral restraints.

88. *for:* as for.

90. *apace:* swiftly.

Now, Esperance! Percy! and set on.
Sound all the lofty instruments of war,
And by that music let us all embrace;
For, heaven to earth, some of us never shall   100
A second time do such a courtesy.

[*The trumpets sound. They embrace, and exeunt.*]

97.   *Esperance!:* Hope! (the battle cry and motto of the Percys).

100.   *heaven to earth:* you can bet heaven against earth.

COMMENTARY

Meanwhile, Worcester and Vernon have returned to the rebel camp. Worcester doesn't want to let Hotspur know about "The liberal and kind offer of the king." Hotspur might accept it, in which case they would all have to spend the rest of their lives under the cloud of suspicion. He acknowledges that the King would be right never to trust them, "For treason but trusted like the fox." Worcester is admitting here that he is like a fox himself, and he says that, although it might be possible for Hotspur's treasons to be excused by his youth and impetuousness, there is no such excuse for the older generation that spurred him on.

This episode shows Worcester at his cynical worst. The King and Hotspur (for all his faults) are motivated by honor; Worcester, selfishly motivated, dishonorably puts a lie between them. This not only makes peace impossible, it seals the fate of his own nephew, Hotspur. Vernon agrees not to pass on the King's offer of peace and pardon, and Worcester tells Hotspur a direct lie: "There is no seeming mercy in the king."

Nothing can stop the battle now. Douglas enters, calling them all to arms. Worcester tells Hotspur of the Prince's offer to fight him in single combat, and Vernon relays how graciously he did so, praising Hotspur's qualities at the same time. Vernon makes it clear how moved he was by the Prince's offer, and speaks warmly of the Prince's promise if he should outlive the day. That the reformed Hal should impress a rebel such as Vernon is evidence of his growing heroic status — a standing that will come to full glory as the warrior-king in Shakespeare's *Henry V*. Hotspur, however, knows only the "libertine" reputation of Prince Hal and is anxious to encounter him in battle.

A messenger arrives with letters for Hotspur, but there is no time to read them. Another messenger announces that the King's advance is rapid. Hotspur is glad to hear that the talking must end and the fighting will begin at last. He utters the Percy family motto, "Esperance!" as a battle-cry, embraces his kinsmen, and exits. His language is full of lofty sentiments, and he speaks of bravery, conscience, justice, and heaven. In short, he faces the prospect of death with honor — the very antithesis of Falstaff's attitude, the expression of which closes the previous scene.

Act V, Scene 3

The fighting has begun. Douglas kills Sir Walter Blunt, believing him to be the King. The Prince comes across Falstaff and asks to borrow his pistol, but his holster only contains a bottle of sack.

ACT V, SCENE 3
Plain between the camps.

[*The* KING *enters with his power. Alarum to the battle.*]

[*Then enter* DOUGLAS *and* SIR WALTER BLUNT.]

Blunt What is thy name, that in the battle thus
  Thou crossest me? what honour dost thou seek
  Upon my head?

Douglas   Know then, my name is Douglas;
  And I do haunt thee in the battle thus
  Because some tell me that thou art a king.   5

Blunt They tell thee true.

Douglas The Lord of Stafford dear to-day hath
    bought
  Thy likeness, for instead of thee, King Harry,
  This sword hath ended him: so shall it thee,
  Unless thou yield thee as my prisoner.   10

Blunt I was not born a yielder, thou proud Scot;
  And thou shalt find a king that will revenge
  Lord Stafford's death.

[*They fight.* DOUGLAS *kills* BLUNT.]

[*Enter* HOTSPUR.]

Hotspur O Douglas, hadst thou fought at Holme-
    don thus,
  I never had triumph'd upon a Scot.   15

Douglas All's done, all's won; here breathless
    lies the King.

Hotspur Where?

Douglas Here.

Hotspur This, Douglas? no: I know this face full
    well:

NOTES

S.D.   *Alarum:* trumpets and drums sounding call to battle.

7–8.   *bought thy likeness:* paid for the fact that he looked like you.

A gallant knight he was, his name was Blunt;　　　20
Semblably furnish'd like the king himself.

Douglas A fool go with thy soul, whither it goes!
A borrow'd title hast thou bought too dear:
Why didst thou tell me that thou wert a king?

Hotspur The king hath many marching in his coats.　　　25

Douglas Now, by my sword, I will kill all his coats;
I'll murder all his wardrobe, piece by piece,
Until I meet the king.

Hotspur　　　　　　　Up, and away!
Our soldiers stand full fairly for the day. [*Exeunt.*]

[*Alarum. Enter* FALSTAFF, *solus.*]

Falstaff Though I could 'scape shot-free at London,　　　30
I fear the shot here; here's no scoring but upon the
pate. Soft? who are you? Sir Walter Blunt: there's
honour for you! here's no vanity! I am as hot as
molten lead, and as heavy too: God keep lead out of
me! I need no more weight than mine own bowels. I　　　35
have led my ragamuffins where they are peppered:
there's not three of my hundred and fifty left alive;
and they are for the town's end, to beg during life.
But who comes here?

[*Enter the* PRINCE.]

Prince What, stand'st thou idle here? lend me thy　　　40
　sword:
Many a nobleman lies stark and stiff
Under the hoofs of vaunting enemies,
Whose deaths are yet unrevenged: I prithee, lend me
　thy sword.

Falstaff O Hal, I prithee, give me leave to breathe
awhile. Turk Gregory never did such seeds in arms　　　45
as I have done this day. I have paid Percy, I have
made him sure.

Prince He is, indeed; and living to kill thee. I
prithee, lend me thy sword.

Falstaff Nay, before God, Hal, if Percy be alive,　　　50
thou get'st not my sword; but take my pistol, if thou
wilt.

21. *Semblably furnish'd:* dressed to resemble the King.

26. *coats:* surcoats, cloth garments with heraldic markings worn over armor to identify the wearer.

45. *Turk Gregory:* Pope Gregory VII, whose reputation for cruelty was like the Turks'.

Prince Give it me; what, is it in the case?

Falstaff Ay, Hal; 'tis hot, 'tis hot; there's that will
sack a city.   55

[*The Prince draws it out, and finds it to be a bottle of sack.*]

Prince What, is it a time to jest and dally now?

[*He throws the bottle at him. Exeunt.*]

Falstaff Well, if Percy be alive, I'll pierce him. If
he do come in my way, so: if he do not, if I come in
his willingly, let him make a carbonado of me. I
like not such grinning honour as Sir Walter hath: 60
give me life: which if I can save, so; if not, honour
comes unlooked for, and there's an end. [*Exeunt.*]

55. *sack:* loot and pilfer; wine of this name.

59. *carbonado:* joint of meat or fish slashed for broiling.

COMMENTARY

The fighting has begun. As in all Shakespearean battle scenes, we see a fast-moving series of little close-up snippets of action in detail rather than large-scale representations from a distance. The action is more or less continuous now, and the scene divisions (which are, in any case, made by editors, not by Shakespeare) become irrelevant. Traditionally, these little incidents follow each other without pause and take place on different parts of the stage. The first encounter we come across is one between Douglas and Sir Walter Blunt. Blunt is one of several on the field who is dressed like the King to deceive the enemy. Douglas believes him to be King Henry, fights with him, and kills him. Hotspur points out to him that he has slain Sir Walter Blunt, "A gallant knight," and that "The king hath many marching in his coats" — that is, in tunics worn over armor to identify the wearer. They move on.

Falstaff comes upon Blunt's body and sees his death as the result of the "honour" he spoke scornfully of at the end of Act V, Scene 1. As for the men in his own company, he has led nearly all of them to their deaths. The three survivors have been so badly injured that they will have to beg for a living. Falstaff has, of course, saved his own skin. As he stands over Blunt's body, the contrast between his cowardice and Sir Walter's honorable self-sacrifice is obvious.

The Prince enters, and finding Falstaff standing idle, calls upon him to lend him his sword: There is much work still to be done. Falstaff asks to be allowed to catch his breath, and refuses to give up his sword. The implication is that Falstaff wants it only to protect himself. He does, however, offer the Prince his pistol, but when Hal opens Falstaff's holster, he finds that it contains a bottle of sack. The jest, symbolic of Falstaff's real priorities, and another play upon the theme of appearance and reality, fails to amuse. The Prince leaves, throwing the bottle at him in contempt, a gesture that emphasizes the growing distance between Hal and his former friends, between the now-dutiful Prince and his past.

Falstaff is left musing on honor again, which he jokingly says might come his way if he happens upon Hotspur, for Hotspur would surely kill him. If that were to happen, it would be an honor "unlooked for." If the choice is between an honorable death and life, Falstaff's preference is plain: "give me life." For all Falstaff's cowardice, we can see his point. Like most of us, he finds himself quite out of place on the battlefield: His only concern is to survive it.

A surcoat, a tunic worn over armor to identify the wearer.
Biblioteca Marciana, Venice, Italy/ET Archive, London/SuperStock

Act V, Scene 4

The Prince saves the King from Douglas, who runs away. Hotspur and the Prince fight. Douglas returns and fights Falstaff, who falls, pretending to be dead. The Prince kills Hotspur and exits; Falstaff gets up and attempts to claim the credit for Hotspur's death.

ACT V, SCENE 4
Another part of the field.

[*Alarum. Excursions. Enter the* KING, *the* PRINCE, LORD JOHN OF LANCASTER, *and the* EARL OF WEST-MORELAND.]

King I prithee,
Harry, withdraw thyself; thou bleed'st too much.
Lord John of Lancaster, go you with him.

Lancaster Not I, my lord, unless I did bleed too.

Prince I beseech your majesty, make up,   5
Lest your retirement do amaze your friends.

King I will do so,
My Lord of Westmoreland, lead him to his tent.

Westmoreland Come, my lord, I'll lead you to your
tent.

Prince Lead me, my lord? I do not need your   10
help:
And God forbid a shallow scratch should drive
The Prince of Wales from such a field as this,
Where stain'd nobility lies trodden on,
And rebels' arms triumph in massacres!

Lancaster We breathe too long; come, cousin West-   15
moreland,
Our duty this way lies; for God's sake, come.

[*Exeunt* LORD JOHN *and* WESTMORELAND.]

Prince By God, thou hast deceived me, Lancaster;
I did not think thee lord of such a spirit:
Before, I loved thee as a brother, John;
But now, I do respect thee as my soul.   20

NOTES

S.D.   *Excursions:* skirmishes, raids.

4.   *make up:* go to the front.

5.   *retirement:* retreat.
           amaze: alarm, dismay.

15.   *breathe:* pause to catch breath.

King I saw him hold Lord Percy at the point
  With lustier maintenance than I did look for
  In such an ungrown warrior.

Prince   O, this boy
  Lends mettle to us all! [*Exeunt.*]

[*Enter* DOUGLAS.]

Douglas Another king! they grow like Hydra's   25
      heads:
  I am the Douglas, fatal to all those
  That wear those colours on them: what are thou,
  That counterfeit'st the person of a king?

King The king himself; who, Douglas, grieves at
      heart
  So many of his shadows thou hast met   30
  And not the very king. I have two boys
  Seek Percy and thyself about the field:
  But, seeing thou fall'st on me so luckily,
  I will assay thee: so, defend thyself.

Douglas I fear thou art another counterfeit;   35
  And yet, in faith, thou bear'st thee like a king:
  But mine I am sure thou art, whoe'er thou be,
  And thus I win thee.

[*They light; the King being in danger, re-enter* PRINCE OF
   WALES.]

Prince Hold up thy head, vile Scot, or thou art
      like
  Never to hold it up again I the spirits   40
  Of valiant Shirley, Stafford, Blunt, are in my arms:
  It is the Prince of Wales that threatens thee;
  Who never promiseth but he means to pay.

[*They fight:* DOUGLAS *flies.*]
  Cheerly, my lord: how fares your grace?
  Sir Nicholas Gawsey hath for succor sent,   45
  And so hath Clifton: I'll to Clifton straight.

King Stay, and breathe awhile:
  Thou hast redeem'd thy lost opinion,
  And show'd thou makest some tender of my life,
  In this fair rescue thou has brought to me.   50

22. *lustier maintenance:* more spirited bearing.

     look for: expect.

24. *mettle:* courage.

25. *Hydra's heads:* In Greek mythology, Hercules slew
     this many-headed monster, which grew two heads
     the moment one of them was cut off.

48. *redeem'd thy lost opinion:* won back your lost
     reputation.

Prince O God! they did me too much injury
  That ever said I hearken'd for your death.
  If it were so, I might have let alone
  The insulting hand of Douglas over you,
  Which would have been as speedy in your end   55
  As all the poisonous potions in the world
  And saved the treacherous labour of your son.

King Make up to Clifton: I'll to Sir Nicholas
    Gawsey. [*Exeunt.*]

[*Enter* HOTSPUR.]

Hotspur If I mistake not, thou art Harry Mon-
    mouth.

Prince Thou speak'st as if I would deny my name.   60

Hotspur My name is Harry Percy.

Prince   Why, then I see
  A very valiant rebel of the name.
  I am the Prince of Wales; and think not, Percy
  To share with me in glory any more:
  Two stars keep not their motion in one sphere;   65
  Nor can one England brook a double reign,
  Of Harry Percy and the Prince of Wales.

Hotspur Nor shall it, Harry; for the hour is come
  To end the one of us; and would to God
  Thy name in arms were now as great as mine!   70

Prince I'll make it greater ere I part from thee,
  And all the budding honours on thy crest
  I'll crop, to make a garland for my head.

Hotspur I can no longer brook thy vanities.

[*They fight.*]

[*Enter* FALSTAFF.]

Falstaff Well said, Hal! to it, Hal! Nay, you shall   75
  find no boy's play here, I can tell you.

[*Re-enter* DOUGLAS; *he fights with* FALSTAFF, *who falls
    down as if he were dead, and exit* DOUGLAS. HOTSPUR
    is wounded and falls.]

Hotspur O, Harry, thou hast robb'd me of my
    youth!

66. *brook:* tolerate.

I better brook the loss of brittle life
Than those proud titles thou hast won of me;
They wound my thoughts worse than thy sword my   80
     flesh;
But thought's the slave of life, and life time's fool;
And time, that takes survey of all the world,
Must have a stop. O, I could prophesy,
But that the earthy and cold hand of death
Lies on my tongue: no Percy, thou art dust,   85
And food for — [*Dies.*]

Prince For worms, brave Percy: fare thee well,
     great heart!
Ill-weaved ambition, how much art thou shrunk!
When that this body did contain a spirit,
A kingdom for it was too small a bound;   90
But now two paces of the vilest earth
Is room enough: this earth that bears thee dead
Bears not alive so stout a gentleman.
If thou wert sensible of courtesy,
I should not make so dear a show of zeal: 95
But let my favours hide thy mangled face;
And, even in thy behalf, I'll thank myself
For doing these fair rites of tenderness.
Adieu, and take thy praise with thee to heaven!
Thy ignominy sleep with thee in the grave,   100
But not remember'd in thy epitaph!

[*He spieth* FALSTAFF *on the ground.*]
What, old acquaintance! could not all this flesh
Keep in a little life? Poor Jack, farewell!
I could have better spared a better man:
O' I should have a heavy miss of thee,   105
If I were much in love with vanity!
Death hath not struck so fat a deer to-day,
Though many dearer, in this bloody fray.
Embowell'd will I see thee by and by:
Till then in blood by noble Percy lie. [*Exeunt.*]   110

Falstaff [*Rising up*] Embowelled! if thou embowel
me to-day, I'll give you leave to powder me and eat
me to-morrow. 'Sblood, 't was time to counterfeit or
that hot termagant Scot had paid me scot and lot
too. Counterfeit? I lie, I am no counterfeit: to die is   115

94.   *sensible of:* aware of.

109.   *Embowell'd:* Disemboweled for embalming.

112.   *powder:* i.e., for embalming or for preserving meat.

114.   *termagant:* violent.

        scot and lot: in full (a phrase equivalent to "lock, stock, and barrel").

to be a counterfeit for he is but the counterfeit of a
man who hath not the life of a man: but to counterfeit dying, when a man thereby liveth, is to be no
counterfeit, but the true and perfect image of life indeed. The better part of valour is discretion; in the   120
which better part I have saved my life. 'Zounds, I am
afraid of this gunpowder Percy, though he be dead:
how, if he should counterfeit too and rise? by my
faith, I am afraid he would prove the better counterfeit. Therefore I'll make him sure; yea, and I'll   125
swear I killed him. Why may not he rise as well as
I? Nothing confutes me but eyes, and nobody sees
me. Therefore, sirrah [*stabbing him*], with a new
wound in your thigh, come you along with me.

[*Takes up* HOTSPUR *on his back*.]

[*Re-enter the* PRINCE OF WALES, *and* LORD JOHN OF
LANCASTER.]

Prince Come, brother John; full bravely hast thou   130
flesh'd thy maiden sword.

Lancaster   But, soft! whom have we here?
Did you not tell me this fat man was dead?

Prince I did; I saw him dead,
Breathless and bleeding on the ground. Art thou
      alive?   135
Or is it fantasy that plays upon our eyesight?
I prithee, speak; we will not trust our eyes
Without our ears: thou art not what thou seem'st.

Falstaff No, that's certain; I am not a double man:
but if I be not Jack Falstaff, then am I a Jack. There   140
is Percy [*Throwing the body down*]: if your father
will do me any honour, so; if not, let him kill the
next Percy himself. I look to be either earl or duke,
I can assure you.

Prince Why, Percy I killed myself and saw thee   145
dead.

Falstaff Didst thou? Lord, Lord, how this world is
given to lying! I grant you I was down and out of
breath; and so was he: but we rose both at an instant and fought a long hour by Shrewsbury clock. If   150

127.   *Nothing confutes me but eyes:* Only an eyewit-
        ness could refute my story.

131.   *flesh'd:* initiated, "blooded."

I may be believed, so; if not, let them that should
reward valour bear the sin upon their own heads. I'll
take it upon my death, I gave him this wound in the
thigh: if the man were alive and would deny it,
'zounds, I would make him eat a piece of my sword.   155

Lancaster This is the strangest tale that ever I
   heard.

Prince This is the strangest fellow, brother John.
   Come, bring your luggage nobly on your back:
   For my part, if a lie may do thee grace,
   I'll gild it with the happiest terms I have.   160

[*A retreat is sounded.*]
   The trumpet sounds retreat; the day is ours.
   Come, brother, let us to the highest of the field,
   To see what friends are living, who are dead.

[*Exeunt* PRINCE OF WALES *and* LANCASTER.]

Falstaff I'll follow, as they say, for reward. He that
   reward me, God reward him! If I do grow great, I'll   165
   grow less; for I'll purge, and leave sack, and live
   cleanly as a nobleman should do. [*Exeunt.*]

159. *do thee grace:* bring credit to you.

160. *gild:* enhance.

166. *purge:* cleanse myself (spiritually or physically, by repentance or by taking drugs to lose weight).

COMMENTARY

The action is continuous from the last scene to this scene. In another part of the field of battle, there are trumpet calls and "excursions" (representations of skirmishes or raiding parties). The King and his two sons, Prince Hal and Prince John, enter with the Earl of Westmoreland. The King tells the Prince of Wales, whom he calls "Harry" (a reminder to the audience that he is a reformed character, and not the fun-loving Hal of the past), to tend to his wounds. The Prince refuses: They are only scratches. His younger brother also refuses to retire. Harry asks the King not to retire either, in case his troops are discouraged. He agrees.

The honor, loyalty, and bravery shown by the King and his two sons, and in which the Prince now takes a leading part, are in direct contrast to the cowardly self-interest of Falstaff that we have only just witnessed. Prince John (of Lancaster) goes off to fight again, and the King and the Prince (of Wales) speak glowingly of his courage.

Douglas now enters, and sees another person dressed as the King, but this time it really is King Henry, who bravely engages him in combat. The Prince comes back to find his father disadvantaged. The Prince challenges, fights, and drives off Douglas, who has so far killed not only Blunt, but also two other valiant lords. King Henry now tells his son "Thou hast redeem'd thy lost opinion." (The word "redeem" has very particular religious associations: It puts the audience in mind of the redeeming self-sacrifice of Christ on the cross, by which mankind was saved. The Prince is a long way from those tavern scenes now.) They speak affectionately to each other, showing them to be united at last. The King leaves to support Sir Nicholas Gawsley, who has sent for help, but before the Prince can go to the aid of Clifton, who is also hard-pressed, Hotspur comes upon the Prince.

The confrontation of Prince Hal and Hotspur is the climax of the play. At this point, the character of these two men is clear: Hotspur is young, brave, and honorable, but hot-headed and rebellious; the Prince is young, brave, and honorable, but (now, at least) wise and dutiful. They acknowledge that there is not room in the kingdom for the two of them as they exchange complimentary challenges. Characteristically, it is Hotspur who tires of talking first and initiates the fighting.

While the audience is watching the dramatic contrast played out between Hotspur and Hal, Shakespeare also reminds us of the difference between Hal as he is now and Hal as he first seemed to be: Falstaff arrives, reminding us of the Prince's past. Douglas turns up, too, and fights with Falstaff, who falls as though dead. The Prince, meanwhile, fatally wounds Hotspur, who dies in the middle of a sentence that has to be completed for him.

The Prince makes a generous funeral speech over the body of "brave Percy." He acknowledges that he had a "great heart" and prays that he should be remembered for his valor, and that the faults of his "ill-weaved ambition" should be forgotten. He then notices the fallen Falstaff, and makes a speech over his body, too. At this critical moment in the play, another key contrast is highlighted. He speaks of Falstaff affectionately ("Poor Jack") but slightingly ("I could have better spared a better man," meaning he will miss him more than he deserves). Hal would miss Falstaff more if he were still in love with "vanity" (that is, with foolishness). Hal leaves, promising that he will have Falstaff "embowell'd" (disemboweled and embalmed).

The prospect of being disemboweled and embalmed brings Falstaff to his feet. He plays with logic again, to defend his cowardly impersonation of death. It is the dead man who is the real deceiver, he says, because a dead man gives the appearance of life without having it; but the man who pretends to be dead when he is alive makes a true image of life, for he preserves both the appearance and reality of life. He follows this comic nonsense with an expression that has become a proverbial justification for those who would rather run away than fight: "The better part of valour is discretion."

There is more comedy when he admits that he fears Hotspur even though he is dead. What if Hotspur is playing the same trick as Falstaff? He makes sure, by stabbing Hotspur's dead body. Falstaff will claim to have killed him. He leaves, carrying Hotspur's body on his back. We can only laugh at his roguery and brazenness. It relieves the tension of the fighting we have just seen, and reminds us that there is something of the coward in all of us. However, it also contrasts keenly with the more noble attitude to matters of life and death that have been shown by both Hotspur and the Prince. We laugh at Falstaff's cynicism, but at the same time we admire the heroism of those he mocks.

The Prince returns with his brother, and they see Falstaff standing, carrying Hotspur's body. They can hardly believe their eyes. Falstaff throws down the corpse, claiming that both he and Hotspur had got up after the Prince had left, and fought for an hour in a fight, which Falstaff won. He points to the wound he gave Hotspur in the thigh, but he doesn't tell them that he made it after Hotspur had been killed by the Prince.

The Prince is pleased to see his old friend alive, even if only for old time's sake. We know from what he said over Falstaff's "dead" body that he now has little regard for Falstaff's foolishness; but, even so, Hal is as charmed by Falstaff's outrageous cheek as we are. The battle is won, and in his joy Hal is perfectly happy to go along with Falstaff's story.

Falstaff is elated, too. Believing that he will be made a noble as a result of his deception, he says that he will give up his self-indulgent ways and become a reformed character. Somehow, Shakespeare does not mean for us to believe him.

Act V, Scene 5

Victory is sounded: The rebel army is defeated. The King orders the execution of Worcester and Vernon. The battle has been won, but civil war is not over yet.

ACT V, SCENE 5
Another part of the field.

[*The trumpets sound. Enter the* KING, PRINCE OF WALES,
LORD JOHN OF LANCASTER, EARL OF WEST-
MORELAND, *with* WORCESTER *and* VERNON *pris-
oners.*]

King Thus ever did rebellion find rebuke.
   Ill-spirited Worcester! did we not send grace,
   Pardon and terms of love to all of you?
   And wouldst thou turn our offers contrary?
   Misuse the tenour of thy kinsman's trust?   5
   Three knights upon our party slain to-day,
   A noble earl and many a creature else
   Had been alive this hour,
   If like a Christian thou hadst truly borne
   Betwixt our armies true intelligence.   10

Worcester What I have done my safety urged
         me to;
   And I embrace this fortune patiently,
   Since not to be avoided it falls on me.

King Bear Worcester to the death and Vernon too: 15
   Other offenders we will pause upon.

[*Exeunt* VERNON *and* WORCESTER *guarded.*]
   How goes the field?

Prince The noble Scot, Lord Douglas, when he saw
   The fortune of the day quite turn'd from him,
   The noble Percy slain, and all his men   20
   Upon the foot of fear, fled with the rest;
   And falling from a hill, he was so bruised
   That the pursuers took him. At my tent
   The Douglas is; and I beseech your grace
   I may dispose of him.   25

NOTES

5.   *tenour:* habitual condition.

8.   *Had:* would have.

10. *true intelligence:* accurate information.

20. *Upon the foot of fear:* fleeing in panic.

King   With all my heart.

Prince Then, brother John of Lancaster, to you
This honourable bounty shall belong:
Go to the Douglas, and deliver him
Up to his pleasure, ransomless and free:
His valour shown upon our crests to-day   30
Hath taught us how to cherish such high deeds
Even in the bosom of our adversaries.

Lancaster I thank your grace for this high courtesy,
Which I shall give away immediately.

King Then this remains, that we divide our power.   35
You, son John, and my cousin Westmoreland
Towards York shall bend you with your dearest
        speed,
To meet Northumberland and the prelate Scroop,
Who, as we hear, are busily in arms: 40
Myself and you, son Harry, will towards Wales,
To fight with Glendower and the Earl of March.
Rebellion in this land shall lose his sway,
Meeting the check of such another day:
And since this business so fair is done,   45
Let us not leave till all our own be won. [*Exeunt.*]

43.   *business:* all three syllables are pronounced.

COMMENTARY

On another part of the battlefield, the rebels Worcester and Vernon have been captured. The King rebukes them for their rebelliousness. Many have unnecessarily lost their lives because Worcester did not convey the King's offer of peace to his opponents. King Henry orders that the two captives be executed. He will make up his mind about what to do with the other prisoners later.

The Prince reports that "The noble Scot, Lord Douglas" has also been captured. He fell down a hill while running away, after seeing that the rebel cause was lost. The Prince asks the King for the right to dispose of him, which he does by setting him free without ransom. This gesture shows that the victors can be merciful and generous to their honorable opponents, as well as justly punishing those like Worcester and Vernon who have behaved dishonorably. Clearly, this royal family is capable of mercy as well as justice. As the play ends, Shakespeare leaves us with the memory of the victorious Henry acting in a very kingly fashion, and his reformed son Hal dutifully supporting him with nobility and grace.

The last speech of the play recalls that though they have won a great battle, they have not yet crushed the rebellion. The King orders Prince John to go with Westmoreland to York, to deal with Northumberland and Scroop, the Archbishop. He and Prince Harry will head for Wales, to tackle Owen Glendower. In this way, Shakespeare reminds us that there is more of the story to be told, and leaves us wanting to hear how it develops in the next play in the series, *King Henry IV, Part 2.*

Notes

Notes

CLIFFSCOMPLETE REVIEW

Use this CliffsComplete Review to gauge what you've learned and to build confidence in your understanding of the original text. After you work through the review questions, the problem-solving exercises, and the suggested activities, you're well on your way to understanding and appreciating the works of William Shakespeare.

IDENTIFY THE QUOTATION

Identify the following quotations by answering these questions:

* Who is the speaker of the quote?
* What does it reveal about the speaker's character?
* What does it tell us about other characters within the play?
* Where does it occur within the play?
* What does it show us about the themes of the play?
* What significant imagery do you see in the quote, and how do these images relate to the overall imagery of the play?

1. My reformation, glittering o'er my fault
   Shall show more goodly and attract more eyes
   Than that which hath no foil to set it off.

2. What, drunk with choler?

3. To put down Richard, that sweet lovely rose,
   And plant this thorn, this canker, Bolingbroke.

4. Banish plump Jack and banish all the world.

5. At my nativity
   The front of heaven was full of fiery shapes

6. I saw young Harry, with his beaver on,
   His cuisses on his thighs, gallantly arm'd
   Rise from the ground like feather'd Mercury

7. What is honour? A word.

8. Two stars keep not their motion in one sphere.

9. Fare thee well, great heart.

10. The better part of valour is discretion.

TRUE/FALSE

1. T F   Worcester is loyal to King Henry.

2. T F   The Hotspur family seat is at Warkworth Castle.

3. T F   Falstaff's horse is stolen by Prince Hal.

4. T F   Owen Glendower speaks no English.

5. T F   " 'Zounds" is an old-fashioned word for "sounds".

6. T F   The name of the Archbishop of York is "Archibald."

7. T F   The real-life Hal and Hotspur were of about the same age.

8. T F   The King before Henry IV was Richard II.

9. T F   At the beginning of the play, there are rebellions in Wales and Scotland.

10. T F   Hotspur's uncle is called "Vernon."

11. T F   Worcester's troops are defeated at the battle of Shrewsbury.

12. T F Douglas is called "The Douglas" to emphasize his bravery.

13. T F Poins is sometimes called "Yedward."

14. T F Gadshill is the name of a character and a place.

15. T F Another name for Prince Hal is "Harry Monmouth."

MULTIPLE CHOICE

1. Lady Mortimer is the daughter of:
   a. Northumberland
   b. Worcester
   c. Owen Glendower

2. Lady Percy is Mortimer's:
   a. sister
   b. mother
   c. aunt

3. Blunt is on the side of
   a. the King
   b. the rebels

4. How many plays are there in a tetralogy?
   a. two
   b. three
   c. four
   d. five

5. The great battle of the play takes place at:
   a. Shrewsbury
   b. Salisbury
   c. Coventry

6. At the beginning of the play, Hotspur displeases the King by refusing to hand over captives he has taken in:
   a. Ireland
   b. Scotland
   c. Wales

7. When the rebels meet in Act III, Scene 1, they divide the map of the kingdom into how many parts?
   a. three
   b. four
   c. five

8. The character with the nose like a lantern is:
   a. Bardolph
   b. Peto
   c. Blunt

9. During the battle, Falstaff is shown to have in his holster:
   a. an unloaded pistol
   b. a pie
   c. a bottle of sack

10. On the morning of the great battle, the weather is:
    a. sunny
    b. snowing
    c. windy

11. Who decides not to pass on the King's offer of peace to the rebels?
    a. Worcester
    b. Vernon
    c. Sir Michael

12. Mistress Quickly's Tavern is in what town?

    a. Charing Cross

    b. Eastcheap

    c. Windsor

13. Who has his pocket picked?

    a. Prince Hal

    b. Peto

    c. Falstaff

14. Who kills Sir Walter Blunt?

    a. Hotspur

    b. Worcester

    c. Douglas

15. At the end of the play, Douglas is:

    a. freed

    b. executed

    c. imprisoned

FILL IN THE BLANK

1. The first scene of the play is set in _____.

2. The last scene of the play takes place near _____.

3. Prince Hal is the Prince of _____.

4. The name of the tavern is _____.

5. _____ is the name of the drawer who is teased by Prince Hal.

6. At the beginning of the play, the King says he wishes that _____ had been exchanged by fairies for his own son when he was a baby.

7. _____'s wife can speak no English.

8. Falstaff claims the credit for the death of _____.

9. Hotspur's dominant "humour" is _____.

10. Hotspur calls Prince Hal "Harry _____", a reference to the town of his birth.

DISCUSSION

Use the following questions to generate discussion:

1. Who are the characters that show heroic qualities in *Henry IV, Part 1*?

2. Account for the comic success of Falstaff, taking into consideration the way that Shakespeare presents all of his faults.

3. How does Shakespeare present the women in this play?

4. What does this play tells us about what it takes to be a good ruler?

5. Why do you think that *Henry IV, Part 1* has always been so popular?

6. Do you find Prince Hal's "reformation" convincing?

7. What do the "tavern scenes" contribute to the success of the play as a whole?

8. Does Hotspur have any attractive qualities?

9. In what sense is *Henry IV, Part 1* a "history" play?

10. How does Shakespeare make this play *exciting*?

IDENTIFYING PLAY ELEMENTS

Find examples of the following elements in the text of *King Henry IV, Part 1*:

* Metaphor

* Simile

* Soliloquy

* Hyperbole

* Idiom
* Prose
* Rhyming Couplet
* Dramatic Irony
* Comedy
* Antithesis

ACTIVITIES

The following activities can springboard you into further discussions and projects:

1. If it is at all possible, see the play performed. Stage performance is what Shakespeare wrote it for, and it's far easier to understand what's going on if you see it acted out than if you have to bring it to life in your imagination when reading it. Even a bad or indifferent or flawed production is worth watching: It might be unsatisfying, but it will leave you thinking about why you were disappointed and how the play should have been produced.

2. Working alone or in a group, design a Web site to help students of *Henry IV, Part 1*. Begin by making a list of what the site should contain, and then sketch out a plan of how the site would work, starting with a home page and deciding how the other pages link together. To make it easy to navigate, be sure that each page has a clear link back to the home page, on which you should provide a contents section. You might choose to include a background section that puts the play in context and perhaps a page for each of the main characters or groups of characters. You could include a summary of the play, scene by scene. Whatever you choose to do, keep in mind the purpose of the exercise: to create a resource that will help someone like yourself who wants to organize his or her thoughts on the play so that they have a firm grasp of it.

3. Imagine that your school is going to put on a production of *Henry IV, Part 1*. Remembering that some of the audience won't have studied the play, that they might be new to Shakespeare, and that they may find his language a little difficult to understand, create a theater program that could help them enjoy and understand the performance. Remember that an audience doesn't have time to read a lengthy introduction: You have to decide what points you want to get across, and make them concisely.

4. Write a script for a short radio program that sets out to explain how the character of Falstaff has come to have such a hold on the popular imagination. You should include short extracts from *Henry IV, Part 1*, and mention the other plays by Shakespeare in which Falstaff appears or is mentioned. You should also find out how Shakespeare finally kills Falstaff off, and consider why he does this.

5. A class or group activity: Stage a mock trial at which Worcester and Vernon are given the opportunity to defend themselves and the rebel cause. Choose students to play the roles of the judge, attorneys, and jury — and include the jury's deliberations as part of the exercise.

6. Research the actual history behind the story of this play. Use history books, encyclopedias and the Internet to help you. Make a list of Shakespeare's deviations from historical fact.

7. Imagine that modern newspaper technology had been available at the time of the play. Produce the front page — and maybe more — of an edition of a newspaper that might have appeared on a key day during the play's events. You will need to appoint an editor and allocate articles, columns and features to members of the group. Before you start, you should spend some time deciding which day from the play to choose.

8. "Balloon Debate": a group or class activity, based upon individual research. Stage a debate in which a number of students take the part of key characters from the play. The idea of a "balloon debate" is that the characters are in the basket of an imaginery hot-air ballon, and that the balloon has only enough power to keep one person safely in the air. Any more than this, and it will crash, and all will be killed. Each character has to make a speech explaining why he or she should be the one to survive, and why the others should be thrown out. The audience participates by asking questions of the characters and then takes a vote on which of them is to be allowed to survive. This can be great fun, but needs a strong chairperson to control it!

9. Individual activity: Choose a character from the play, and write a full description of his or her personality from two points of view: first, as if written by a friend and admirer; second, as if by an enemy. Justify your comments by close reference to the text of the play. Then consider your own response to the character, and how Shakespeare has encouraged that response in you.

10. Individual, then group activity. Select a few characters in the play. Choose *one* short quotation (made by or about them) that you think best sums up their characters as revealed in the play. Compare results, and take a vote, if you wish, on which is the best quote for the job.

ANSWERS

Identify the Quote

1. Speaker: Prince Hal; Person spoken to: He speaks these lines to himself, so that the audience of the play can hear him thinking aloud. It is a soliloquy; Location: Act I, Scene 2; Comments: The lines are taken from the Prince's speech at the end of Act I, Scene 2, in which he declares that he is not as he seems. Hal is, at heart, a responsible character, and he believes that, when he shows his real virtuous self to the people, they will admire him all the more for its contrast with his previous reputation.

2. Speaker: Northumberland; Person spoken to: Hotspur; Location: Act I, Scene 3; Comments: This short accusation of uncontrollable anger sums up one of Hotspur's dominant characteristics. It is all the more convincing because it is spoken by a father to a son.

3. Speaker: Hotspur; Persons spoken to: Northumberland and Worcester; Location: Act I, Scene 3; Comments: These words sum up the intensity of hatred that the Percys feel towards the usurping King, against whom they rebel and who they believe has no right to reign.

4. Speaker: Falstaff; Person spoken to: Prince Hal; Location: Act II, Scene 4; Comments: This is the scene in which Hal and Falstaff take turns acting out the interview that they imagine will take place between Hal and his father. Falstaff is here playing the role of the Prince, and putting the case strongly that Hal should be allowed to keep his friendship with Falstaff. The importance of the speech is greater than its comedy. As the play goes on, it becomes increasingly clear that Hal and Falstaff are growing apart, and this affectionate banter will be a thing of the past. In *Henry IV, Part 2*, Hal does indeed reject his old friend outright.

5. Speaker: Owen Glendower; Person spoken to: Hotspur; Location: Act III, Scene 1; Comments: Glendower's language here marks him out as self-important (like Hotspur) but with an almost mystical, fanciful imagination (very unlike Hotspur's). This quote underlines the incompatibility of the two rebels.

6. Speaker: Vernon; Persons spoken to: Hotspur, Worcester, and Douglas; Location: Act IV, Scene 1; Comments: This enthusiastic description of the figure cut by the Prince is all the more impressive because it comes from the mouth of one of his enemies. The *hyperbole* (a literary term meaning "exaggeration") of its expression presents Hal (who is here called, more respectfully, "Harry") as if he were a kind of god.

7. Speaker: Falstaff; Person spoken to: He speaks these lines to himself, so that the audience of the play can hear him thinking aloud. It is a soliloquy; Location: Act V, Scene 1; Comments: This speech is an important one given by Falstaff, in which he expresses his contempt for the notion of honor, at a time when a great battle is about to take place in which many men will *die* for honor, and his friend, Prince Hal, will be one of those fighting for it. This soliloquy takes us to the very heart of Falstaff's character, showing the audience how he and the Prince are growing apart.

8. Speaker: The Prince; Person spoken to: Hotspur; Location: Act V, Scene 4; Comments: The sentence neatly sums up the rivalry of the two contrasting and competing young heroes.

9. Speaker: The Prince; Person spoken to: Hotspur, already dead; Location: Act V, Scene 4; Comments: This shows how the Prince is magnanimous in victory, showing respect for the courage and honor of the man it has been his duty to kill.

10. Speaker: Falstaff; Person spoken to: He speaks these lines to himself, so that the audience of the play can hear him thinking aloud. It is a soliloquy; Location: Act V, Scene 4; Comments: This neat excuse for Falstaff's cowardice has become proverbial. It is another contrast with the courage of those around him, including the fallen Hotspur and the Prince who killed him.

True/False

1. False 2. True 3. False 4. False 5. False 6. False 7. False 8. True 9. True 10. False 11. False 12. False 13. True 14. True 15. True

Multiple Choice

1. c 2. a 3. a 4. c 5. a 6. b 7. a 8. a 9. c 10. c 11. a 12. b 13. c 14. c 15. a

Fill in the Blank

1. London (The Palace) 2. Shrewsbury 3. Wales 4. The Boar's Head 5. Francis 6. Hotspur 7. Mortimer 8. Hotspur 9. Choler 10. Monmouth

CLIFFSCOMPLETE RESOURCE CENTER

The learning doesn't need to stop here. CliffsComplete Resource Center shows you the best of the best: great links to information in print, on film, and online. And the following aren't all the great resources available to you; visit www.cliffsnotes.com for tips on reading literature, writing papers, giving presentations, locating other resources, and testing your knowledge.

BOOKS, MAGAZINES, AND ARTICLES

Bullough, Geoffrey. *Narrative and Dramatic Sources of Shakespeare: Later English History Plays: King John, Henry IV, Henry V, Henry VIII.* New York: Columbia University Press, 1962.

Really keen scholars may want to look up the sources used by Shakespeare and see for themselves how he has adapted them — and this book provides the opportunity to do just that. *Note:* This is probably a book to borrow from the library rather than to buy; at the time of writing its price is $99.

Doyle, John and Ray Lischner. *Shakespeare For Dummies.* Foster City, California: IDG Books Worldwide, Inc., 1999.

This guide to Shakespeare's plays and poetry provides summaries and scorecards for keeping track of who's who in a given play, as well as painless introductions to language, imagery, and other often intimidating subjects.

Shakespeare, William. *Four Histories: Richard II/Henry IV, Part One/Henry IV, Part Two/Henry V.* New York: Penguin Classics, 1995.

Those who would like to read the whole story, of which this play forms one part, can do so in this volume.

INTERNET

Illinois Shakespeare Festival

(www.orat.ilstu.edu/shakespeare/shakespeare.html)

This site has an attractively presented range of resources, including some very helpful essays on plays produced. "The Making of a King: Henry IV, Part 1" by Kim Pereira is a well-written piece that many students find accessible and helpful.

Mr. William Shakespeare and the Internet

(daphne.palomar.edu/shakespeare/)

This site has many good links to every kind of resource and aims to be a complete annotated guide to the scholarly Shakespeare resources available on the Internet. It also includes many resources of more general use, such as details of Shakespeare festivals.

Webspeare

(cncn.com/homepages/ken_m/shakespeare.html)

This site is aimed particularly at high school students. Among its many useful and attractive features is a section devoted to teaching the proper pronunciation of Elizabethan English, with easily downloaded sound files as examples.

The Works of the Bard

(www.gh.cs.su.oz.au/~matty/shakespeare/shakespeare.html)

This site offers free downloadable copies of the plays, some of them with very good search engines that can help identify or find quotations or references. An interesting use of such a facility would be to find out the number of times that certain key words are used in the play, for example.

FILMS

Chimes at Midnight, known also as *Falstaff*. Directed by Orson Welles. Performed by Orson Welles and John Gielgud. 1965.

This film is a fascinating adaptation of much of *Henry IV, Part 1* and some of *Henry IV, Part 2*. It is marvelous cinema but hard to come by. Students new to either play should be aware that Welles makes many cuts and changes that may be confusing. Among its many insights is a brilliant characterization of Falstaff by Welles himself.

BBC Television Shakespeare: Henry IV, Part I. Directed by David Giles. Performed by Anthony Quayle, Jon Finch, and David Gwillim. 1979.

This made-for-television movie is true to the text and has an excellent cast, including Anthony Quayle as Falstaff. It brings the play convincingly to life but finding a copy of the film is difficult.

Hal. Directed by Christopher T. Parks. Performed by John Ahlin, Stevie Ray Dallimore, Les Minski, and Chris Guild. 1998.

This film is a more recent conflation of both of Shakespeare's plays about Henry IV. It is easily available in video format from Muse of Fire Films, P.O. Box 247, East Brunswick, New Jersey 08166 (e-mail: **onewiz@aol.com**).

Henry V. Directed by Laurence Olivier. Performed by Laurence Olivier, Renee Asherson, Harcourt Williams, and Robert Newton. 1944.

This famous version of *Henry V*, directed by and starring the classic Shakespearean actor Laurence Olivier, is worth watching for its charming recreation of an original Elizabethan theater in the early part of the film. It also, of course, shows the full glory achieved by Prince Hal of *Henry IV, Part 1* when he becomes king himself.

Henry V. Directed by Kenneth Branagh. Performed by Kenneth Branagh, Derek Jacobi, Simon Shepard, James Larkin, Brian Blessed, James Simmons, and Emma Thompson. 1989.

Those who would like to see a less romanticized version of *Henry V* (when compared to the 1944 Olivier version) should watch this more recent version made by Kenneth Branagh.

OTHER MEDIA

SHAKSPER Listserv

(SHAKSPER@ws.bowiestate.edu)

This Listserv is an international electronic conference for Shakespearean researchers, instructors, students, and those who share their academic interests and concerns. For further details, e-mail the moderator, Dr. Hardy M. Cook, at **SHAKSPER@ws.bowiestate.edu**

Shakespeare, William. *Henry IV, Part 1*. Audio cassette. New York: Penguin Audiobooks, 1999.

A first-class (but slightly abridged) audio recording of the play has been produced by Penguin Audiobooks. The cast includes Jamie Grover as Prince Hal and Richard Griffiths as Falstaff. Those who find Shakespeare's language difficult to understand at first can be greatly helped by following the text while listening to a good tape like this.

CLIFFSCOMPLETE READING GROUP DISCUSSION GUIDE

Use the following questions and topics to enhance your reading group discussions. The discussion can help get you thinking — and hopefully talking — about Shakespeare in a whole new way!

DISCUSSION QUESTIONS

1. Although *Henry IV, Part I* is a history, it has both tragic and comic scenes and characters. Are tragedy, comedy, and history three separate genres? In what way are tragedy and comedy aspects of history? What might Shakespeare be saying by combining tragic, comic, and historical elements into one play?

2. *Henry IV, Part I* features a large cast of supporting characters. Why did Shakespeare include the characters of Poins? Bardolph? Lady Percy? Glendower? Vernon? What do these characters add to the play? How would the play be different if you took away each of these characters?

3. *Henry IV, Part I* is often performed with the two plays that follow it — *Henry IV, Part II* and *Henry V.* When performing multiple plays, casting the role of Hal (who eventually become Henry V) presents some challenges. *Henry IV, Part I* needs a youthful Hal, but the strength and emotional scenes in the later plays require an experienced (and often older) actor. What are the pros and cons of casting a younger actor as Hal? What about an older actor? Do you need to cast one actor to do all three plays? Or would multiple actors be more appropriate?

4. While Falstaff and the tavern folk speak mainly in bawdy prose, the royal court speaks mainly in verse. How does Hal's speech change when he is in both worlds. Does Hal communicate better in one world over another? What might Shakespeare be saying about how language creates our world? Or how our world creates our language?

5. Falstaff is a thief, a liar, a drunkard, a glutton, a cheat, and a coward — and yet the best actors throughout the ages have longed to play him, and audience and readers are fascinated by him. What makes this character so interesting? How comically do you think he should be played? How darkly?

6. Many films and stage productions have set other Shakespearean plays in time periods and locations different from those specified by Shakespeare in his original writing. For example, productions of *Julius Caesar* have been set in Nazi Germany, a 1930s Chicago meatpacking factory, and even in outer space. Although *Henry IV, Part I* is rooted in history, can it be set in other time periods or locations? What would be lost by setting the play in time period different from it historical roots? What might be gained? What characters, lines, or scenes would need to be cut or rewritten to fit with changes in time period or location?

7. Most of Shakespeare's original audience was already familiar with the character of Hal because numerous "wild prince Hal" stories where part of the *national mythology* of

England. In most of these stories, Hal is reckless and wild — a free spirit. What characteristics does Shakespeare add to Hal, in order to give him more depth and complexity? What national mythology exists for other famous leaders? How does national mythology affect our understanding of the past?

8. Although Hal's development is the dramatic continuity of the play, many actors prefer to play Hotspur. Why might this be so?

9. Although historians are not certain of the exact date when *Henry IV, Part I* was first performed, Queen Elizabeth would have been well into her sixties and did not have an assured heir to the throne. While *Henry IV, Part I* isn't purely a political play, it was written during a passionate political era. What about the play feels politically anxious? What are the play's hopeful, more reassuring aspects?

10. In a sense, Hal is a student in the classroom of life. He studies in the royal court, on the battlefield, and in the tavern. What do each of these "classrooms" bring to Hal's education? Does Hal balance what he has learned? Does Shakespeare believe in a balanced education for leaders?

11. In a recent U.S. production, the roles of Falstaff and Henry were played by the same actor. (The moments where both characters appear together, required the use of a body double and sound recordings.) What are the pros and cons of the doubling? What does the play lose? What does it gain?

12. Robert Bly's popular book about the men's movement, *Iron John,* refers frequently to *King Henry IV, Part I.* How is Hal's journey the journey that all men go through? How are the influences in his life (Henry, Hotspur, Falstaff, and so on) the influences that all men encounter?

Notes

Notes

Index

Notes

CliffsNotes™

CLIFFSCOMPLETE
Hamlet
Julius Caesar
King Henry IV, Part I
King Lear
✓ Macbeth
✓ The Merchant of Venice
Othello
✓ Romeo and Juliet
The Tempest
✓ Twelfth Night

Look for Other Series in the CliffsNotes Family

LITERATURE NOTES
Absalom, Absalom!
The Aeneid
Agamemnon
Alice in Wonderland
All the King's Men
All the Pretty Horses
All Quiet on Western Front
All's Well & Merry Wives
American Poets of the
    20th Century
American Tragedy
Animal Farm
Anna Karenina
Anthem
Antony and Cleopatra
Aristotle's Ethics
As I Lay Dying
The Assistant
As You Like It
Atlas Shrugged
Autobiography of Ben Franklin
Autobiography of Malcolm X
The Awakening
Babbit
Bartleby & Benito Cereno
The Bean Trees
The Bear
The Bell Jar
Beloved
Beowulf
Billy Budd & Typee
Black Boy
Black Like Me

Bleak House
Bless Me, Ultima
The Bluest Eye & Sula
Brave New World
Brothers Karamazov
Call of Wild & White Fang
Candide
The Canterbury Tales
Catch-22
Catcher in the Rye
The Chosen
Cliffs Notes on the Bible
The Color Purple
Comedy of Errors…
Connecticut Yankee
The Contender
The Count of Monte Cristo
Crime and Punishment
The Crucible
Cry, the Beloved Country
Cyrano de Bergerac
Daisy Miller & Turn…Screw
David Copperfield
Death of a Salesman
The Deerslayer
Diary of Anne Frank
Divine Comedy-I. Inferno
Divine Comedy-II. Purgatorio
Divine Comedy-III. Paradiso
Doctor Faustus
Dr. Jekyll and Mr. Hyde
Don Juan
Don Quixote
Dracula
Emerson's Essays
Emily Dickinson Poems
Emma
Ethan Frome
Euripides' Electra & Medea
The Faerie Queene
Fahrenheit 451
Far from Madding Crowd
A Farewell to Arms
Farewell to Manzanar
Fathers and Sons
Faulkner's Short Stories
Faust Pt. I & Pt. II
The Federalist
Flowers for Algernon
For Whom the Bell Tolls
The Fountainhead
Frankenstein
The French Lieutenant's Woman
The Giver
Glass Menagerie & Streetcar
Go Down, Moses

The Good Earth
Grapes of Wrath
Great Expectations
The Great Gatsby
Greek Classics
Gulliver's Travels
Hamlet
The Handmaid's Tale
Hard Times
Heart of Darkness & Secret Sharer
Hemingway's Short Stories
Henry IV Part 1
Henry IV Part 2
Henry V
House Made of Dawn
The House of the Seven Gables
Huckleberry Finn
I Know Why the Caged Bird Sings
Ibsen's Plays I
Ibsen's Plays II
The Idiot
Idylls of the King
The Iliad
Incidents in the Life of a Slave Girl
Inherit the Wind
Invisible Man
Ivanhoe
Jane Eyre
Joseph Andrews
The Joy Luck Club
Jude the Obscure
Julius Caesar
The Jungle
Kafka's Short Stories
Keats & Shelley
The Killer Angels
King Lear
The Kitchen God's Wife
The Last of the Mohicans
Le Morte Darthur
Leaves of Grass
Les Miserables
A Lesson Before Dying
Light in August
The Light in the Forest
Lord Jim
Lord of the Flies
Lord of the Rings
Lost Horizon
Lysistrata & Other Comedies
Macbeth
Madame Bovary
Main Street
The Mayor of Casterbridge
Measure for Measure
The Merchant of Venice

Middlemarch
A Midsummer-Night's Dream
The Mill on the Floss
Moby-Dick
Moll Flanders
Mrs. Dalloway
Much Ado About Nothing
My Ántonia
Mythology
Narr. …Frederick Douglass
Native Son
New Testament
Night
1984
Notes from Underground
The Odyssey
Oedipus Trilogy
Of Human Bondage
Of Mice and Men
The Old Man and the Sea
Old Testament
Oliver Twist
The Once and Future King
One Day in the Life of
    Ivan Denisovich
One Flew Over Cuckoo's Nest
100 Years of Solitude
O'Neill's Plays
Othello
Our Town
The Outsiders
The Ox-Bow Incident
Paradise Lost
A Passage to India
The Pearl
The Pickwick Papers
The Picture of Dorian Gray
Pilgrim's Progress
The Plague
Plato's Euthyphro…
Plato's The Republic
Poe's Short Stories
A Portrait of the Artist…
The Portrait of a Lady
The Power and the Glory
Pride and Prejudice
The Prince
The Prince and the Pauper
A Raisin in the Sun
The Red Badge of Courage
The Red Pony
The Return of the Native
Richard II
Richard III
The Rise of Silas Lapham
Robinson Crusoe